EATING
WILD
IN EASTERN
CANADA

Dandelion greens

EATING WILD IN EASTERN CANADA

A GUIDE TO FORAGING THE
FORESTS, FIELDS, AND SHORELINES

JAMIE SIMPSON

NIMBUS
PUBLISHING
— NIMBUS.CA —

Nimbus Publishing Limited
3660 Strawberry Hill St., Halifax, NS, B3K 5A9
(902) 455-4286, nimbus.ca
Printed and bound in Canada
NB1320

Design: Kate Westphal, Graphic Detail

Library and Archives Canada Cataloguing in Publication
        Simpson, Jamie, 1974-, author
        Eating wild in Eastern Canada : a guide to foraging the forests, fields, and shorelines / Jamie Simpson.

        Issued in print and electronic formats.
        ISBN 978-1-77108-598-4 (softcover).
        —ISBN 978-1-77108-599-1 (HTML)

1. Wild foods—Atlantic Provinces. 2. Wild plants, Edible—Atlantic Provinces. 3. Seafood gathering—Atlantic Provinces. 4. Cooking (Wild foods). 5. Cookbooks. I. Title.

TX823.S52 2018   641.3009715   C2017-907979-4
                                  C2017-907980-8

Nimbus Publishing acknowledges the financial support for its publishing activities from the Government of Canada through the Canada Book Fund (CBF) and the Canada Council for the Arts, and from the Province of Nova Scotia. We are pleased to work in partnership with the Province of Nova Scotia to develop and promote our creative industries for the benefit of all Nova Scotians.

*To my mum, who gave me
free rein (benign neglect?) to
roam woods and shorelines as
a kid, gamely cooked rabbits,
grouse, and a porcupine that
I brought home, and once
made me periwinkle pizza.*

Beach peas

Table of Contents

Chapter 3 | Seashore and Intertidal Areas   95

Part 1: Sea Plants

Soft-shell clams

Bayberry

Acknowledgements

Thanks go to my botanist friend (and rock-climbing adventure partner) Rich Lapaix for checking the botanical names of plants in this book. Any remaining errors are mine. Thanks go to friends Alain Belliveau, Christopher Majka, Dan Hutt, and Jennifer MacLatchy for generously contributing photographs, advice, and information. Thanks also to my partner, Eleanor, for contributing photographs, encouraging foraging adventures, and sportingly sampling many wild foods. A special thank you goes to the many friends who make foraging trips fun and meaningful. Finally, I thank Nimbus Publishing for seeing merit in a book about wild edibles, and Kate Kennedy for her expert and artful editing skills.

Highbush cranberry

Introduction

A lazy December morning found my partner and me chatting idly with my old friend Wyatt as we lingered over a lobster breakfast. My friend fishes from a small boat on the Passamaquoddy Bay, and he'd grabbed three of the previous day's catch for our meal. Several cups of coffee after the lobster, we decided a walk was in order to forestall complete laziness.

The day was winter grey and spruce green until a shrub heavy with lively red berries caught our attention. *Viburnum opulus.* Highbush cranberries. Having no basket or sack, I put my toque to use and gathered a hat-full of the partially frozen berries. We tried a few straight from the shrub, our faces puckering a little at their sour juice. Although they're not a cranberry at all, their cranberry colour and tartness earned them their misnomer.

Our guilt assuaged, we walked home and recommenced our chatting, drinking, and eating. I dropped the clusters of berries into a saucepan with a touch of water and brought them to a gentle simmer before mashing them with a fork. A few minutes more and I dumped the slurry into a colander to let the liquid separate from the large seeds. On the stove again, I added sugar until the juice was only playfully, seductively tart, and then brought it to the table. Tentatively, Wyatt dipped a little chunk of bread in the red juice. Hmm, better than the fresh berries, he commented. Eleanor added a little sharp cheddar cheese to her hunk of bread before dipping it. Now we're on to something, she said. The sweet and tart of the sauce matched the sharp cheese and the bread mellowed both. Before long we were looking at an empty bowl.

I've been fortunate to share many such moments with friends: finding, cooking, and enjoying everything from periwinkles to partridgeberries, mushrooms to mackerel. Adventurous and tasty, eating wild gives us a new awareness of our natural world. From fiddleheads to spruce tips to edible seaweeds, wild foods open our eyes to the culinary potential held in the fields, forests, and shorelines near our homes. Woodlands yield golden chanterelles. Soft-shell clams lie a few centimetres below the surface of tidal flats. Barrens and rocky shorelines can abound with cranberries and huckleberries.

Many wild edibles have short seasons, but there is almost always something to be gathered whatever the time of the year. Every May I tingle with anticipation of walking riverside, crouched low, filling bags with bright green fiddleheads. On summer forest hikes I sneak sideways glances for the yellow glow of chanterelles. Digging soft-shelled clams for a late fall dinner is my ultimate treasure hunting. In winter the highbush cranberry's cheerful red catches my eye against the season's greys and whites, and sprigs of white pine are available year-round to make a lemony tea.

Gathering edibles is instinctive. Most kids take to it with the barest encouragement. Friends almost invariably widen their eyes and smile when I introduce them to a chanterelle in the forest for the first time. For much of humankind's existence, gathering (and hunting) was daily life. For a few hundred thousand years, generation after generation spent part of their days gathering food. For thousands of years, until just a couple of hundred years ago, the Mi'kmaw, Maliseet, and Passamaquoddy peoples of what is now eastern Canada lived entirely from their knowledge of the plants and animals of this land.

For a few, wild food is more than a hobby, even today. Like my lobster-fisher friend, some gather, trap, or hunt wild food to supplement their income or their kitchens. Chanterelles and fiddleheads are sold to restaurants and at farmers' markets. Rare is the tidal flat not pocked by a commercial clamdigger's hoe. During a year I spent in Newfoundland, I met many who filled their freezers with moose, berries, and cod caught or gathered by themselves or friends and family.

Huckleberry

For most of us, though, gathering wild food is nothing more or less than enjoying a few relaxing hours in the woods or along the shore and bringing home an interesting treat for the dinner table. For me, life's stresses lift when I'm on the hunt for chanterelles or filling a basket with cranberries. My thoughts wander with my feet and my shoulders relax. I am rewarded with far more than mushrooms or berries for my effort.

This book is a tour of the plants, fungi, animals, and algae that I think are fun to find and gather, and a pleasure to prepare and eat. By no means is this book comprehensive —consider it a primer to whet your appetite (and wet your feet). There will be many more foraging possibilities to explore when you're done here. The edible wild foods in this book are loosely grouped by where you will likely find them: the forests, the fields, rivers and bogs, and the shorelines. Naturally, habitats overlap. Many berries for example grow in fields *and* along shorelines.

Over time, those who gather wild food build up mental notes of their favourite foraging sites. Some folks may share such knowledge, but don't be surprised if the information is held close. It's a rite of passage to seek and find one's own places to gather. I hope this book will point you in the right direction for specific foods, and remember that the "treasure hunt" for wild foods is part of the fun.

Beach pea

Bayberry

Chanterelles and a bolete

Chicken-of-the-woods

The Traditional Word of Caution

"Thank you for not poisoning my wife," he said to me following a hike I took with a group of friends along a section of Newfoundland's East Coast Trail. Along the walk, I had introduced my companions (including my friend's wife) to a variety of berries, leaves, and mushrooms, all of which were new to them. Hesitant at first, everyone eventually joined the trail-side tasting and later took home a bag of chanterelle mushrooms.

Most of us have a knee-jerk reaction to berries and mushrooms we don't know: danger! True, there are some plants and some mushrooms that can make us sick and some that can kill us. Shellfish can become contaminated with toxins. Don't take these dangers lightly. Fortunately, with a little knowledge and appropriate research you can avoid them. It should go without saying that no one should ever eat a wild edible without being certain of what it is. Notes are provided throughout this book on some potential dangers. That said, a blanket fear of wild edibles is entirely unreasonable and unnecessarily limits a worthwhile adventure into nature's culinary riches.

About Names

To my chagrin, botanists change the names of plants from time to time. It's hard enough to learn them once. Highbush cranberry, for example, has been *Viburnum trilobum* in my mind ever since my botany course at Acadia University, but the correct nomenclature is now *Viburnum opulus*. Others have similarly been changed over the years, and I've done my best to account for these changes.

Chapter 1

Forests and Edges | Fungi, Trees, Shrubs, and a Few More

Part 1: Fungi

Chaga

Chanterelle

Black Trumpet

Winter Chanterelle

Matsutake

Oyster Mushroom

Boletes

Chicken-of-the-Woods

Lobster Mushroom

How do you pick the right mushroom? Hunting mushrooms with a knowledgeable friend, attending a fungus-identification course, and using a fungus guidebook are all good ways to start. Using a guidebook alone might not be enough. In any event, learn your mushrooms before you cook them. Start with a few easily identifiable mushroom species and eat only a small portion of a mushroom until you are certain you know which kind you have picked and that you do not have an allergy to it. Although easily avoidable with a basic understanding of mushroom identification, people are occasionally poisoned when they mistakenly pick and eat the wrong mushroom species. That said, with reasonable caution there is no need to be paranoid about wild mushrooms.

Picked mushrooms need air so avoid stuffing them into plastic bags. Paper bags are okay and a wooden basket is best. Avoid rinsing them with water. It's better to cut, scrape, or brush any dirt or debris off the mushroom to avoid having the mushroom soak up water. Collecting during dry weather tends to result in cleaner mushrooms with less water content and thus better flavour and texture. When slicing your found fungi, discard any soft or mushy bits and any bits compromised by insects.

Perhaps the best way to prepare wild mushrooms is the simplest: sauté them lightly in butter. That's how I usually enjoy my chanterelles, although adding a piece or two of bacon is never a bad idea. Many wild mushrooms are excellent additions to pasta dishes and soups too. Some wild mushrooms, including chanterelles, dry well and can be stored for months in a cool, dry place. The first species in this section, however, is not eaten at all. This fungus—chaga—is just for tea.

Chaga (*Inonotus obliquus*)
a.k.a. Cinder Conk, Birch Conk, Clinker Polypore

"Like dark chocolate, but without the sweetness," my friend mused, sipping her first cup of hot chaga tea. "So, like unsweetened chocolate?" I asked. "No, there's no bitterness. It's chocolate, without the bitter or the sweet, and the aftertaste of an Americano," she offered.

For me, chaga is liquid birch trees. Those lucky enough to have cut and split birch firewood, either white or yellow birch, likely know that fresh birch smell that you can almost taste. A little sweet, a little spearmint, a little earthy. I'll often pause while splitting birch just to pick up a piece and enjoy its scent. It's worth splitting a cord of birch firewood just for that smell. Chaga tea is that smell condensed into a hot beverage.

Chaga doesn't look like a fungus and chaga tea doesn't taste like fungus. It looks like burnt charcoal and when you crack it open it's orange-brown on the inside. Chaga grows on white and yellow birch trees, usually in fist-sized to head-sized bumpy black clumps. Oddly, I once found it growing on an ironwood tree, although perhaps this is not as odd as one might think given that ironwood belongs to the birch tree family. Chaga is found throughout eastern Canada and around the world wherever birch trees grow, from Russia to Europe to the northern United States. Chaga grows slowly, so take only a little from any one area. Unfortunately it is reported to be over-harvested in some regions.

Chaga has been used to make tea and as a folk medicine for centuries in Russia and other northern countries. The fungus can be simply broken into small chunks and steeped to make tea or can be ground in a coffee grinder and used with a tea infuser. I steep five or six small chunks—no more than a small handful—in a couple litres of water. It's fully steeped once the water turns dark, and it doesn't seem to mind sitting around for a day or two with the pot lid on. Just reheat it when you want a cup. Chaga also doesn't seem to get too strong no matter how long it steeps, and I find I can replenish the water once or twice and still have a flavourful tea. Sometimes I add a splash of milk and a bit of honey for a comforting nighttime beverage.

David Spahr, author of *Edible and Medicinal Mushrooms of New England and Eastern Canada*, reports that he had great success adding concentrated chaga tea to an India pale ale he brewed. He boiled down the chaga tea to concentrate it, added it to his brewing wort instead of hops, and thoroughly enjoyed the resulting beer. A few commercial craft-brewers have caught onto the beer-chaga combo, too, and chaga lagers and porters are starting to appear at craft breweries.

Those interested in the possible therapeutic effects of chaga should do a bit of research on preparation methods. Hot water steeping releases some of the good stuff. Other methods are more effective at releasing other compounds.

The best way to locate chaga is to take a long hike through mature mixed forest or hardwood forest that has some birch trees (white or yellow) and scan all the birches you come across. Chaga is generally found on older birch trees so don't bother with young forests, and make sure the birch tree is alive as the fungus doesn't live long on dead trees. To harvest, use a hatchet or axe to remove a portion of the fungus from the tree if you can reach it; otherwise continue your quest. Don't take an entire clump of chaga —leave at least half to ensure the fungus can regrow—and be careful not to wound the tree by cutting into it. All other mushrooms we collect are the fruiting structures of the underground body of the fungus known as mycelium. The chaga we collect, however, is the very body (mycelium) of the fungus, which is why it's important to leave at least half still attached to the tree.

Cut freshly harvested chaga into small chunks with a heavy knife and set them near a sunny window or other mild heat source to dry. Once chaga dries it becomes much more difficult to cut, so do it soon after harvesting. Summer chaga has higher water content, so chaga harvested during the cooler months is easier to dry.

Chanterelle (*Cantharellus cibarius* and other species)

Photo by Christopher Majka

Offer someone wild mushrooms and he may turn up his nose. Offer the same person chanterelles and he may gratefully accept. With their apricot aroma, al dente texture, and unique flavour, chanterelles bridge the worlds of foragers and grocery-store-only types.

I have collected chanterelles for many years, but a favourite recent memory is a hike with friends along the East Coast Trail in Newfoundland. My friends' eyes sparkled when I pointed out a patch of yellow under the fir and spruce trees. "Chanterelles? Really?!" With an almost obsessive vigour our leisurely hike became a chanterelle hunt. "Ben's got gold fever bad," his wife remarked, as Ben called urgently from a newly discovered patch. We selected ones with firm flesh and little evidence of insect damage and made sure to leave some unpicked. Empty lunch bags and toques were put into service to hold the fungus and we momentarily forgot about our hike.

Chanterelles comprise a number of similar species, and as a group are found in many parts of the world, including Europe, North America, Asia, and part of Africa. I often find them growing under spruce trees, or in mixed-wood forests that include spruce and birch. The largest patches I have found were growing on old pasture land that had grown up in spruce trees. They often seem to appear in or along the sides of old roads or trails in these types of forests. I can't remember finding them in pure hardwood forests, but perhaps I just haven't looked enough.

Chanterelles are among those fungi species that form intimate connections with trees and are known as mycorrhizal fungi. The main body of chanterelles and other fungi species live underground, spread out in a wide network of filaments known as mycelium. The chanterelle's mycelium grows into the tiny root hairs of certain tree species, enabling carbohydrates to flow from the tree to the fungus, and water and minerals to flow from the fungus to the tree. It's like the fungus giving the tree an extended network of roots to access what it needs in exchange for some food that the tree makes from sunlight. A good deal all around.

Finding chanterelles

Look for yellow V-shaped fungi with gill-like irregular ridges that run almost all the way down the "trunk" or stipe of the fungus. Importantly, these ridges are not uniform like true mushroom gills. If they are uniform, then it's not a chanterelle. Chanterelles also have a particular aroma, which many describe as fruity or apricot-y. Chanterelles range in width from one to ten centimetres or more. Smaller chanterelles often have a convex (sort of umbrella-like) top, while larger ones often grow into a funnel or vase (concave) shape.

Importantly, not all yellow or orange mushrooms are chanterelles. The jack-o-lantern and the false chanterelle mushrooms (reportedly poisonous) may be similar in colour and shape, but each of these has well-developed, uniform gills that never fork, unlike the chanterelle. As with any plant or mushroom, the best way to learn to identify a chanterelle is to have a knowledgeable person show you. Once you've seen a few, you shouldn't have any trouble recognizing its distinctive beauty.

Chanterelles are better picked when they are dry (not immediately after rain), so that they do not contain excess water. Once in a while I have to cut off part of the stipe to get rid of buggy bits, but chanterelles are typically bug-free. I come across chanterelles from late June to late September (sometimes into October), with the best picking often in July and early August. The size of patches varies from year to year, but I can count on going back to favourite spots year after year to find at least some to bring home.

My chanterelles tend to quickly find themselves in a frying pan with a little butter. Many flavours in chanterelles are fat-soluble and some are alcohol-soluble, so adding a touch of wine when sautéing in butter, oil, or cream can be a nice addition. You can also cook them in a little bacon fat. Just don't cook them too long. A couple of minutes in a hot pan is plenty.

To dry chanterelles, slice them in halves or quarters and place the slices by a sunny window or in an oven on very low heat. Store your dried chanterelles in a glass jar and crumble them into soups or pasta sauce for flavouring, or soak them in water to rehydrate them and add as a pizza topping. For those interested in the health benefits, chanterelles are reportedly high in vitamins C and D, and potassium.

Black Trumpet (*Craterellus cornucopioides* and other species) a.k.a. Horn of Plenty, Blank Chanterelle

Black trumpets and winter chanterelles

Black trumpets, a cousin of the common chanterelle, can be tricky to find given their small stature and colour that blends well with the forest floor. If you are not looking for them specifically you may easily overlook them. I first happened on some when I was leaning against a tree for a rest while hiking though a mixed hardwood and softwood forest in southwestern Nova Scotia. Glancing down I noticed a couple of the delicate fungi near my feet. With their image in my mind, I walked around a bit and was surprised to find them scattered throughout that part of the forest.

Black trumpets are usually some three to ten or so centimetres high and have a vase or trumpet shape with a hollow stipe (stem) and thin flesh. They do not have gills but rather have either smooth outer flesh or hints of ridges in place of gills. Black trumpets grow in the shade of mature forests from mid to late summer, and are often found where rain or snowmelt washes through a forest in the spring.

My first meal of black trumpets was like tasting a delicious tropical fruit for the first time, and they immediately jumped to first place in my list of favourite wild mushrooms. They are worth the hunt. I suggest sautéing them in a little butter, on their own, to ensure you get their full flavour. Mycophile David Fischer suggests letting a few soak in white wine for a couple of days and then drinking the wine (and cooking the soaked mushrooms). I intend to try this with the next black trumpets I find.

Winter Chanterelle (*Craterellus tubaeformis* and other species) a.k.a. Yellow Foot

Once upon a time, winter chanterelles resided with the chanterelle group of mushrooms. Then a discerning mycologist picked apart their genetic building blocks, found they were merely masquerading as chanterelles, and promptly shuffled them into the *Craterellus* group. Such are the fickle nuances of mushroom nomenclature.

Winter chanterelles have yellow stems that are partially hollow, and yellow, orange, or dark brown caps that often have a distinct "innie" bellybutton-like hole. I have found them in mature conifer and mixed-wood forests, often with red spruce or hemlock, from late summer until they are covered by snow.

I think they are best enjoyed sautéed by themselves so as not to lose any of their delicate flavour, but you can also add them to creamy soups and pastas.

Matsutake (*Tricholoma magnivelare*)
a.k.a. Pine Mushroom

Photo by Alain Beliveau

Matsutake mushrooms are perhaps best known for their popularity in Japan (although those that grow in Japan may be a different species—or not; scientists argue the point). Poems are written, stories told, and large amounts of money spent, all for the love of the matsutake mushroom.

Matsutake is a late summer and fall mushroom that likes to grow among hemlock trees, especially on slopes and sometimes near streams or lakes. Not an easy mushroom to find, it seems to be associated with certain types of soils, particularly podzol or spodosol soils, which can be identified by the presence of a grey soil layer immediately under the forest floor.

They emerge from the forest floor looking like white balls being pushed up out of the soil. Important: *Do not* assume any emerging white mushroom is edible. Some are deadly poisonous. Ensure that you correctly identify any white mushroom or it may be your last meal.

How to cook matsutake? This can be an art in itself, and if you want to move beyond my "butter and salt" approach you would be well advised to dive into your own research. Perhaps the best place to start would be with recipes from the matsutake heartland: Japan.

Oyster Mushroom (*Pleurotus ostreatus, P. populinus*, and other species)

In spring and summer, *populinus* can be found growing on dead poplar (aspen) trees. In fall to early winter, *ostreatus* can be found on living sugar maple and occasionally other hardwood trees including beech. Oyster mushrooms can be from three to over twenty centimetres wide, and are white to tan to brown in colour. They are fleshy (*not* woody or inflexible), they do not have noticeable stems, and they grow only on wood (never out of the ground).

Don't confuse oyster mushrooms with angel wings (*Pleurocybella porrigens*), which are thin white fungi that grow on conifer trees. While many resources list them as edible, some reports suggest that angel wings are poisonous to some people.

Sauté oyster mushrooms in butter or oil and enjoy by themselves or add them to a stir-fry. Some people like to cook them in a tempura batter.

Bolete (*Boletus edulis* and many other species)

Boletes commonly grow with hemlock, oak, or spruce and can be found in most forest types from early summer into the fall. All boletes have pores under their caps instead of gills or other structures. The pore structures of most boletes are whitish or yellow in colour. It is best not to pick any boletes with red or orange pore structures as some of these species may be poisonous or otherwise unpleasant to eat. As with any wild mushroom, it is best to pick with an experienced mushroom picker when foraging for boletes.

There is also the bitter bolete. It resembles edible boletes except in taste: it is staggeringly bitter. I know this because my mycology professor at Acadia University (Professor Grund) asked our class for a volunteer to taste a bit of one, and in the interest of experiential learning I raised my hand. Never again!

Boletes can be added to stir-fries or enjoyed sautéed on their own or with other wild mushrooms. They can be dried like chanterelles.

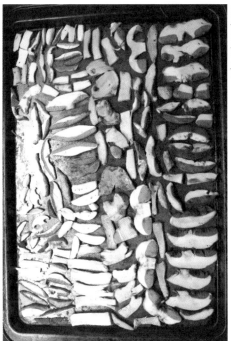

Photo by Christopher Majka

Chicken-of-the-Woods (*Laetiporus sulphureus, L. cincinnatus*)

Chicken-of-the-woods usually grows in hardwoods and is easily spotted thanks to its colour—from bright orange to orange-yellow to pale yellow—and its overlapping layers of caps. It grows out of dead or mature hardwood trees.

These mushrooms can grow tough and disagreeable in flavour as they age, so seek out the youngest chicken-of-the-woods you can find. They can be sautéed, added to soups, or baked in the oven.

Lobster Mushroom (*Hypomyces lactifluorum*)

The lobster mushroom is an interesting beast. It is a parasitic fungus that attacks either of two species of fungus (*Lactarius piperatus* or *Russula brevipes*), overthrows their bodies, and transforms them into a shape and colour that we recognize as the lobster mushroom. Luckily for us, this transformation also turns these otherwise unpalatable mushrooms into culinary delights.

Why are they called lobster mushrooms? They have a colour that is similar to that of cooked lobster, and when they are cooked they smell and taste a little like seafood. Look for them in mixed hardwood and softwood forests during late summer and early fall. Cutting your lobster mushroom at ground level rather than tearing it out will help keep its mycelium intact and able to sprout another "lobster."

Do not bother picking any lobster mushrooms that are soggy or largely eaten by critters. When sliced open, they should be pure white on the inside; discard any that are not. They are lovely cut into strips or steaks and fried, or try adding them to a seafood chowder.

Spruce tips

Our eastern forests are nothing if not diverse. Thanks to a wide range of bedrock and soil types, along with a varied geography and ocean influences, eastern forests are comprised of more than thirty species of trees and dozens of unique tree-community types. An hour's drive could easily take you through half a dozen different forest communities.

Importantly for the forest forager, many wild edibles are associated with specific forest communities. There's little sense in searching for cucumber root, for example, in a coastal spruce and balsam fir forest, or for fiddleheads in a black spruce bog. Knowing your prey's habitat is the first step in successful foraging. The second step is to always keep your eyes open for various target habitats you may encounter while hiking or driving and take the time to stop and explore these potential foraging hot spots.

Forest edges, whether along old agricultural fields or the margins of ponds and rivers, often abound with wild edibles. Wild cherries, highbush cranberries, serviceberries, hawthorns, sumacs—all of these and more live in the transition zone between field and forest. Edges are their niche. Hedgerows are a sort of artificial forest edge and offer excellent foraging opportunities.

Deep forest tends to offer fewer wild edibles save for mushrooms, although cucumber root is a notable exception. It thrives in the low-light conditions of mature hardwood and mixed hardwood-softwood forests, usually in rich soils. Bunchberry too is a forest dweller and sometimes carpets forest floors. Why do we say "deep" when talking about forests? My guess is that it is the same reason we say deep when talking about under-water environments, where sunlight is diminished. The sunlight that reaches the forest floor is sometimes too little to support an abundance of plant growth, so when foraging in the forest, look for the sunnier spots.

Conifer Tips and Teas: Spruce (*Picea* species), Balsam Fir (*Abies balsamea*), Pine (*Pinus* species), and Hemlock (*Tsuga canadensis*)

In late spring and early summer, the tips of conifer trees are a light green colour, distinct from the darker green of mature needles. These tips are surprisingly tender and can be nibbled raw. Each species has a characteristic flavour: hemlock is my favourite, with an almost lemony taste, and balsam fir is the most bracing with its acerbic nip.

Conifer tips can be gathered and eaten for as long as they remain tender and light green in colour. Just pluck them from the branch with your fingers, or use scissors if you prefer. Be sure to pick enough tips to store a bunch (sealed in bags or jars and frozen) for later use. Once they mature (turn dark green and are no longer tender), they are good only for tea (see next page). The youngest tips may still have a brown, papery bud sheath, which is easily pulled off.

What to do with your haul of green tips? Minced conifer tips added to mayonnaise can give your sandwiches a perky, woodsy twist. Try substituting conifer tips for rosemary, or throwing some conifer tips into whatever stew or soup you have on the go. Conifer tip vinegar is made by covering tips with boiling hot vinegar (white or cider). Put the vinegar and tips into jars, let mellow for a week or longer, and enjoy.

White pine tea

Conifer tip syrup is made by covering tips with a boiling water and sugar mix, using equal volumes of tips, water, and sugar, and letting sit for a few hours or overnight. The strained liquid (that is, the syrup) can be stored in the fridge and used with carbonated water to make a cool drink, or as an ingredient in experimental cocktails.

Alaskan chef Laurie Constantino, described by some as the Queen of Spruce Tips, recommends using some of your spruce tip syrup to make candied spruce tips. Prepare the syrup as above, then add a cup of spruce tips and bring to a boil. Let simmer for a couple of minutes and then remove from heat and let cool before straining the syrup from the tips. Keep the syrup in the refrigerator for other uses, and sprinkle the spruce tips with granulated sugar. Place the tips on waxed paper with space between each and allow to dry (which may take a couple of days). Once dry, store in an airtight container in the refrigerator.

Spruce tip beers have been brewed for centuries. I've had the good fortune to try spruce tip beer brewed commercially in Cape Breton and in Alaska. Both were excellent. For home brewers, add a few handfuls (100–200 grams or so) of spruce tips to your wort, and experiment with amounts to suit your taste. Older recipes for spruce tip beer are a bit more primitive but perhaps worth a try for adventurous brewers. Here's a recipe from Joseph Banks's 1766 journal of his travels in Newfoundland, adapted from Kitty Drake's 1994 cookbook *Rabbit Ravioli*:

> *Take a copper [pot] that contains [holds] 12 gallons. Fill it as full of the boughs of black spruce as it will hold, pressing them down pretty tight. Fill it up with water. Boil it till the rind [bark] will strip off the spruce boughs, which will waste [reduce] it about one-third. Take them out and add to the water one gallon of melasses [molasses]. Let the whole boil till the melasses are disolvd. Take a half hogshead [barrel—likely 32 gallons in size] and put in 19 gallons of water and fill it up with the essence [the water boiled with boughs and molasses]. Work it with barm [likely brewer's yeast] or beergrounds [your guess is as good as mine] and in less than a week it is fit to drink.*

Conifer tips can be easily stored by packing them into a glass jar with a sealed lid and freezing them. For an aromatic treat, do this with balsam fir tips and then open up the jar once in a while just to inhale their scent.

The twigs and needles of pine, spruce, balsam fir, and hemlock make a nice tea at any time of year. Simply break off a handful of live twigs with their needles attached, throw them in a pot of water, bring to a boil, and let steep for a moment. I like white pine tea the best. It has a surprisingly pleasant lemony taste. Other pine species might be just as good, but I have yet to try them. Conifer needle tea is reportedly high in vitamin C, and was used in times past to avoid scurvy during winter. Sadly, a number of Samuel de Champlain's men died from scurvy during the winter of 1604 on St. Croix Island (near what is now St. Andrews, New Brunswick), when a cure for the disease was growing all around them.

Note: Pick only from forest trees. Yew is a common ornamental shrub and occasional forest shrub that could be confused for a young conifer tree and is poisonous.

Spruce Tip Rice Tarts
(Makes 10)
By George Smith and Cora-Lea Eisses-Smith

2 pints of milk
7 ounces short-grain rice
3.5 ounces ground almonds
10 ounces candied spruce tips, crumbled (recipe to follow)
3 whole eggs
5 egg yolks
Zest ½ lemon
Butter and fine bread crumbs with which to line tins

Preheat the oven to 350° F.

Cook the rice in the milk until tender, and then allow it to chill. Stir in all the other ingredients.

Butter 10 individual tart tins, line with the fine bread crumbs, and divide the mix evenly between them.

Bake in the oven for 25-35 mins, or until firm. Cool before removing from tins.

Serve drizzled with spruce tip syrup.

Candied Spruce Tips and Syrup
(Makes 2 cups of syrup)

4 tightly packed cups of spruce tips
2 cups sugar
2 cups water

Place all ingredients in a pan over low heat and simmer for 10-15 mins.
Leave to cool and infuse for 6 hours or longer.

Strain the syrup, retaining the spruce tips. Place the spruce tips in a dehydrator for 2-3 hrs.

Return syrup to the heat to reduce, until the syrup turns a dark amber colour.

Store any leftover syrup in the fridge, and any leftover spruce tips at room temperature in an airtight container.

Edible Trees: Red Oak Acorns (*Quercus rubra*), Beech Leaves and Nuts (*Fagus americana*), and Maple Leaves (*Acer* species)

There is a sweet spot in early summer, about two weeks long, starting just after beech leaves unfurl from their buds, when they can be eaten like salad greens. The same goes for maple leaves. These leaves can also be cooked like spinach or added to soups.

Beech tree

Beech nuts

Photo by Tom Rogers

Beechnuts were once collected every autumn by the bushel. The fat-rich nuts provided fall sustenance to Mi'kmaq and colonists alike, along with black bears, ruffed grouse, and numerous other wildlife species. Unfortunately, a disease inadvertently introduced from Europe—the beech bark disease—has reduced the abundance of large, healthy beech trees that produce large nut crops. Nonetheless, a few beechnut-producing trees can still be found and collecting their bounty is a fun fall adventure.

Some beechnut collectors place a sheet or blanket under trees with heavy crops of nuts and wait for the nuts to fall and fill the blanket. Others comb through the fallen leaves below beech trees searching out the fallen treasures. Some climb the trees to pick a pocketful. Heavy crops come only every few years, so it's worth checking groves of beech trees year to year. Beechnuts are encased in a triangular, somewhat spiny husk that is removed to reveal a pair of beechnuts. The shell can be opened with a thumbnail to get at the meat of the nut. Eat them raw or roasted and sprinkled with salt.

If you see a beech tree with a mess of broken branches high in its canopy you can bet a bear has been feasting. Bears sit themselves on a solid beech limb and then pull nut-loaded branches to themselves, often breaking them in the process.

Our native oak, the red oak, is another oily-nut-producing tree that feeds many of our wildlife species in autumn. Acorns from red oak trees have high amounts of tannins and are not as easy eating as beech nuts. Boiling the shelled acorn meats in a few (or more) changes of water can make them somewhat palatable. Once leached of their tannins, the meats can be eaten as is or ground into bits and cooked as a porridge. Or dry them and then grind them into flour. If not used right away, store the meats (ground up or whole) in the fridge or freezer to prevent the oil in the acorn from turning bad. How to shell an acorn? Some use a knife, some bash them with a hammer, and some dry them in a pan on low heat to make them easier to split open.

If you spot a tiny hole in the side of the acorn, you should chuck it in the woods. Unfortunately, acorns are favoured by a weevil (a small insect) that renders them useless for food, and the hole is a telltale sign that the acorn is no longer worth collecting (for food or for growing oak trees).

Highbush Cranberry (*Viburnum opulus*)

Highbush cranberry shrubs are often found along the edges of fields and roads. The red, juicy, tart berries may remind you of cranberries, but cranberries they are not. Highbush cranberry, despite the name, belongs to the *Viburnum* genus, unrelated to the cranberry family.

Highbush cranberries grow in large clusters that are satisfying to pick. The berries are always rather tart, but slightly less so after a frost or two, and they often remain on the shrubs into the winter, making it possible to collect them even when snow covers the ground.

I always nibble a few highbush cranberries when I see them just to remind myself of how tart they are and then immediately stop. I like to boil them until the juice is liberated from the flesh and seeds, adding a touch of water if necessary to keep them from burning (usually they have enough of their own liquid to make this unnecessary). A little mashing helps this process. Then I strain the boiled berries and add sugar or other sweetener to the liquid. Once a little sweet is added, the underlying flavour of the highbush cranberry comes through. You might marvel at its addictive flavour and completely forget the puckering taste of the raw berry.

Add the syrup to porridge, use it as a dip for bread, or pour it over ice cream. Add pectin and turn it into a jelly. If you can separate out the seeds (a food mill helps), the pulp can be made into a tasty spread so long as you add a little sugar or other sweetener.

Wild Raisin (*Viburnum nudum*)

The changing colour of wild raisin berries, from white to pink to red to dark blue, marks the transition from summer to autumn for me. The sun might still yield warmth, but dark blue wild raisin berries mean the door has closed on summer and I shift gears to thoughts of short days and frosty nights.

Wild raisin berries are sweet, completely in contrast to their highbush cranberry cousin, and are lovely to nibble on once they are ripe (dark blue). Just remember that they have a large seed that must be spit out. Wild raisins can be gathered, cooked in a pot with a little water, and strained to remove the seeds to make an interesting syrup. Add pectin to make it into a jelly.

Common Elderberry (*Sambucus canadensis*) a.k.a. Black Elderberry

I appreciate a berry that can be gathered quickly. Although only a few millimetres wide, the fruit of common elderberry grows in large clumps and often at a convenient height for picking, so the trick is stopping before you have too many. Ripe once they are dark blue or purple (almost black), the berries have a touch of sour that some people might not take to at first taste.

Common elderberry often grows in rich soils that are a bit wet. Roadsides and edges of fields are common habitats and some people plant them as ornamental shrubs. In June they produce gorgeous clusters of creamy white flowers (which are edible before and after they open, and can be steeped to make a pleasant tea), and the fruit is ripe by late summer or early fall. The pith is easily removed from elderberry stems, leaving a hollow tube that can be used to make a whistle. Search the Internet for elderberry whistle instructions.

Some enjoy eating elderberries raw for their peculiar flavour; others make jam and jelly with them, sometimes adding the juice of other fruit or berries (they have no pectin themselves). They freeze well and add a zip of vitamin A and C to cereal and porridge throughout the winter.

To make elderberry flower syrup, put the flowers of half a dozen flower clusters in about a litre of water, bring to a boil, and immediately remove from heat. Let sit for a few hours before straining out the flowers and adding two or three cups of sugar. Bring back to a boil and let simmer for half an hour. Keep in the refrigerator and use in desserts or add water (sparkling if you like) for a summery, sweet drink. Put a few elderberry flowers into your ice-cube tray when making ice cubes to add a flourish to your summertime drink.

For elderberry flower fritters, just dip the flower clusters into your favourite pancake batter and panfry or deep-fry until brown.

"And your father smelled of elderberries," taunted the French soldier in *Monty Python and the Holy Grail*. Elderberries do have an interesting smell, but perhaps the soldier was referring to their common use for making wine. In *Weeds of the Woods*, his excellent book on shrubs, Glen Blouin includes the following recipe for elderberry wine:

Pour four cups of boiling water over four cups of crushed elderberries and let sit for four days before straining and adding four pounds of sugar. Stir and let sit another four days. Add two sliced lemons and two sliced oranges. Dissolve one package of yeast in four tablespoons of water and pour this over a slice of toast. Float the toast on the berry juice and let sit (you guessed it) four more days (or longer). Strain, bottle, and let sit four weeks or more.

Red-berried elder (*Sambucus racemosa*) is another species of elderberry native to eastern Canada. As the name suggests, its berries are bright red when ripe. Although birds will eat the berries, they are reportedly poisonous for humans.

Common elderberry flowers

Wild Apple (*Malus* species)

To appreciate the wild and sharp flavours of these October fruits, it is necessary that you be breathing the sharp October or November air....This noblest of fruits must be eaten in the fields, when your system is all aglow with exercise, when the frosty weather nips your fingers, the wind rattles the bare boughs or rustles the few remaining leaves....What is sour in the house a bracing walk makes sweet.—Henry David Thoreau in *Wild Apples*

I once mentioned to an early girlfriend my dedication to sampling all wild apples. I meant it literally, but she took it metaphorically, and soon left me for other pursuits!

Wild apples are not native to North America, but rather have naturalized themselves in old fields, roadsides, and hedgerows, feral and often forgotten. Cultivated apples are produced through cuttings to maintain nearly exact genetic replication. The seeds of these cultivated varieties, however, store memories of their origins. Trees that grow from these seeds express some of their wildness, and apples from these trees are a roll of the genetic dice.

In my experience, wild apples range from utterly inedible to surprisingly satisfying. Some can be eaten with relish from the tree, some are good for a bite or two, some can only be considered once cooked and tamed with a generous application of sugar. All wild apples can be transformed into jelly or apple butter. As they contain pectin, the juice from wild apples can be added to the juice of other fruit or berries to help set jellies.

Wild apples make excellent apple sauce, and can also be baked with meat roasts. Remove the cores manually, or simply cut up and cook the apples and then strain the cooked mush through a strainer to remove the seeds and bits of core. If you can get your hands on a food mill, it takes a lot of the work out of making apple sauce. Just chop the apples, remove any rotten bits, and cook (skin, core, and all). Once mushy, run the cooked apples through the food mill and presto: apple sauce separated from seeds and skin. Add sugar and perhaps cinnamon and lemon juice to taste.

Rum and wild apples make a pleasing jelly. Cook enough wild apples to make three cups of juice, add a cup of rum, three cups of sugar, and a pouch of pectin to the juice, bring to a boil and pour into sterilized jars. For apple-mint jelly, substitute a cup of wild mint leaves for the rum.

If you live on a property with wild apple trees, consider giving them some room by cutting away competing shrubs and trees. You can also prune dead branches and thin dense clusters of branches to improve the tree's health. Even if you do not reap their bounty, a host of birds and other wildlife will. To convince your neighbours that you've completely gone off the deep end, you might consider reviving the old tradition of wassailing—visiting your fruit trees in the early new year, banging pots with sticks and singing songs to encourage plentiful fruit come summer.

Here's a wassailing chant that your trees may like:

We wassaile our trees, that they may beare
Us many an Apple and many a Peare:
For more or lesse fruits they will bring,
As we do give them Wassailing.

Serviceberry (*Amelanchier* species)
a.k.a. Wild Pear, Indian Pear, Saskatoon, Shad Bush, Juneberry

Photo by Patrick Bürgler

In May, the serviceberry's rush of white blossoms enlivens otherwise drab roadsides and field edges. In mid– to late summer, its sweet fruit ripen to a deep purple. In fall, the leaves turn scarlet. Spring to fall, serviceberry is a fine sight.

Sweet, juicy, and flavourful, serviceberries are best eaten directly from the tree. At least I cannot resist eating them that way. I cannot imagine being disciplined enough to collect a pie's worth, or even a jar of jam's worth, without eating them all long before I return to my kitchen. But those who can stop themselves from eating them immediately report that serviceberries make an excellent pie and excellent jam.

Unfortunately, a berry this good does not last long. Birds and other animals seem to gobble ripe serviceberries the day before I intend to pick them. Insects can damage the berries making them unpalatable. If you manage to gather a good crop of serviceberries, it's something to celebrate.

One of this tree's common names is shad bush. Shad (a type of fish) migrate up rivers around the same time as this tree blossoms in the spring. One explanation for the serviceberry name is that its flowering signals the point in the spring when the ground is thawed enough to hold a burial service for anyone who died over the winter months.

Chokecherry (*Prunus virginiana*) and Pin Cherry (*Prunus pensylvanica*)

Chokecherry and pin cherry blossoms follow close on the heels of serviceberry's bloom and the berries are ripe in the late summer and early fall. The fruit of both pin cherry and chokecherry give you a dry mouth, and are mainly eaten by children (and childlike adults) who wish to test how far they can launch the cherry pits from their mouths after chewing off the sour cherry flesh. Be careful not to swallow the pits as they can cause an upset stomach; cherry tree leaves are similarly poisonous.

Pin cherries and chokecherries grow in clusters and are easily picked in quantity, although pin cherries are smaller and usually sparser. Cherry juice for sipping (on its own or mixed with rum) or jelly can be made by cooking the cherries with a covering of water until the fruit is soft, then mashing them before straining the juice through a mesh sieve to remove the pits. The colour of the juice alone is almost worth the effort. Add sugar or other sweetener to taste and to counter the dry-mouth effect. Combine with juice from wild apples to make an apple-cherry jelly. Just remember, choke and pin cherries are mostly pit, so collect more than you think you'll need (a few litres at least) in order to make enough juice to do something with.

A lovely drink can be made by filling a glass jar three-quarters full of chokecherries, adding vodka to fill the jar, letting it sit for a few weeks (shaking it now and then if you remember), mashing the berries with a potato masher, and then straining the liquid to remove the pits. The drink has a dangerously rich and satisfying cherry flavour without any of the dry sourness of raw chokecherries or the harshness of straight vodka.

You can make a playful vinegar by pouring boiling-hot white vinegar over a pot of cherries, then covering the pot with a towel and waiting a week. Mix and mash the berry-vinegar mix during the week whenever you think of it, then strain off the liquid and add sugar to taste. Bring the liquid to a boil and then store in sealed sterilized jars or bottles. Use the vinegar in salad dressing or meat dishes. To make a tasty fizzy drink, Blanche Garrett, author of *A Taste of the Wild*, suggests combining one part cherry vinegar with three parts soda water and adding sugar or other sweetener if necessary. Garrett also suggests mixing cherry syrup (cherry juice mixed with sugar), port, and brandy in equal parts, and then heating—but not boiling or simmering—to make cherry negus.

Mountain Ash (*Sorbus americana* and other species) a.k.a. Rowan, Dogberry in Newfoundland and Labrador

After trees have lost their leaves, and cold winds are foretelling winter, the rocky hillsides around St. John's, Newfoundland, are cheered with dabs of orange. Called dogberry in Newfoundland, and rowan in Europe, mountain ash are at home along hardscrabble coastlines and other marginal soils throughout eastern Canada. Their large clusters of orange berries add welcome colour to otherwise drab November days.

Springtime clusters of small white flowers are followed by green berries that gradually gain colour over the summer. The berries are not palatable at all until after a few frosts, and even then are not particularly favoured as a raw berry. In any event, they should not be eaten in any quantity when raw as they contain compounds that can cause indigestion. Cooking, however, neutralizes these compounds.

Mountain ash berries can be cooked either by themselves or with wild apples to make jelly. Add just enough water to cover the fruit, bring to a boil, and simmer for twenty minutes or so. Strain the liquid from the fruit (through jelly cloth if you like clear jelly), add a cup of sugar for each cup of liquid, and bring to a boil. Simmer until a spoonful of the liquid jells when placed on a plate that is set in the freezer for a moment, and then put into sterilized jars.

Mountain ash is an ash only in name. It is not part of the ash family, but rather belongs to the rose family along with apples and cherries.

Staghorn Sumac (*Rhus typhina*)

A relative of mangos and cashews, sumac looks almost tropical with its flashy arrays of leaflets, twisty stems, and upright, horn-like clusters of red berries. Sumac grows in old fields and hedgerows and along roadsides and forest edges, never reaching more than seven or so metres high, and are often shorter. Its characteristic clusters of berries and its younger twigs are covered in tiny hairs, giving sumac a velvety appearance.

In late summer, the clusters of ripe berries can be collected to make a lemonade sort of drink. Cover the berries with boiling water and let them sit for twenty minutes or so before straining the liquid through a couple of layers of cheesecloth to remove the hairs. You definitely don't want the little hairs in your summer's afternoon drink. Add sweetener to taste. The liquid can also be made into jelly, either on its own or in combination with other fruits or berries.

Sumac is also collected to make a seasoning. Collect a few clusters of the berries, separate them from their cluster, and let them dry for a few days. Once the berries are dry, use a blender or food processor to rough them up. The purpose of the blender is to knock the tiny bit of dried flesh away from the berry's large seed. There's not much flesh on a sumac berry, but a little sumac seasoning goes a long way. Once the seeds have lost most of their red flesh, dump the seeds and flesh into a mesh strainer and mix them about to encourage the fine red bits to sift into a container below. Try it on roasted potatoes or broiled chicken. Ever wonder what gives za'atar its characteristic zip? Yep, sumac.

Hawthorn (*Crataegus* species)

Thorns and haws are what this shrub is all about. No other shrub in eastern Canada has the awl-like thorns of the hawthorn, which were once used as sewing needles and are hard enough to puncture thin leather. The shrub's abundant haws (fruit) resemble miniature apples, and although seedy and not particularly tasty they can be eaten raw once ripe in the fall. The haws can also be made into jam or jelly by boiling and mashing them with a little water, straining to remove seeds, then boiling again with a cup of sugar per cup of liquid before storing in sterilized jars. Hawthorn haws have a long history of use for their reportedly medicinal value, particularly for heart and circulatory system health.

Photo by Christopher Majka

Cucumber Root (*Medeola virginiana*)

Crisp, cool, and juicy, cucumber root is a perfect snack when you stop for a rest during a long canoe portage on a warm summer's day. Unfortunately, eating cucumber root kills the plant, so only enjoy a few and avoid picking any unless you see an abundance of the plants in the area.

Cucumber root tends to grow in rich soils, often in mature hardwood and mixed-wood forests. Look for the distinctive whorls of elliptical leaves, then dig some three to ten centimetres into the earth below the stem. Following the stem will lead you to a small white tuber. Brush off the dirt and enjoy it right there and then. Save some for a friend if you have the willpower. If you find a large patch of cucumber root, you can pick a handful to add to a salad.

Bunchberry (*Cornus canadensis*)

The sheer abundance of these little orange forest-floor berries entices hikers to try them. Inevitably a few are eaten and the rest are summarily passed over once the hiker remembers why she never really liked eating bunchberries.

Bunchberries have a mild (some might say bland) taste and seeds that need to be crunched before swallowing. There is no real substance to the berry's flesh and so the annoying seeds are the most memorable part of the experience. They are a lovely little forest floor plant, though, and are the smallest of the dogwood family. And as unimpressed with their taste as I inevitably am every single time, I cannot help but grab a handful whenever I see them along a walking trail.

Wintergreen (*Gaultheria procumbens*)

Wintergreen grows low to the ground in mixed-wood forests and scrubby barren areas with acidic soils. Its bright, shiny green leaves and red berries are unmistakable. As its name suggests, its leaves often stay green year-round (although sometimes they turn rusty reddish).

The berries are the best part of the plant and can sometimes be found in late winter or spring as the snow recedes, having survived the winter and still offering a taste of sweet wintergreen flavour. New berries come along in late summer and early fall and are ripe once they are bright red. The leaves can be chewed for a while for their wintergreen flavour and then spit out.

Wintergreen tea can be made from the leaves (the pale-green new leaves are best) and from the berries.

Fred Dardenne, originally from Belgium, is a professional wild food forager living near Halifax, Nova Scotia. Fred offers wild food workshops, sells fresh seasonal wild foods, and makes several wild food products for sale year-round.

Some people say to me, "Your life is a dream." It's not always a dream. It's a lot of hard work and long hours, and sometimes in terrible weather. And a lot of driving. Last year I drove sixty thousand kilometres around Nova Scotia on my foraging trips. Of course, I have to think about my family too, and make sure I'm making enough of a living. But yes, a lot of the time it really is a dream, I think. I love it. Ever since I was a boy growing up in Belgium, I have wanted to be out in nature.

When I was young, I used to go fishing a lot, and every time I went I recorded notes about the weather. Eventually I knew the best weather for a given season to catch fish. Now, I apply the same approach to finding mushrooms. I record the weather, date, and the types of trees where I find mushrooms and it works well. Mushrooms are the most challenging wild food to understand. After ten years of hunting mushrooms I'm starting to understand them!

I work about six to eight months a year, full-time. For now my work is very seasonal but I'm creating products that I can sell year-round. I've started pickling sea rocket pods, for example. They're very tasty and it's a product that I can sell in the winter, along with dried seaweeds, juniper berries, and others.

In the summer season I sell about a hundred pounds of product a day to restaurants, distilleries, local shops, and also to buyers in Ontario and Quebec, mostly Toronto and Montreal. I'm hoping to expand my market into Europe as well. I gather approximately two hundred kinds of wild food products: mushrooms, seaweeds, plants, lichens, spices, berries. Sea lettuce is a very popular item now. If I had a thousand pounds of it right now I could sell it. Every chef wants it these days. I also buy from other foragers, maybe forty or fifty other foragers who like to do a little bit of foraging here and there.

Most wild foods have a very short season for picking, when they are at their best quality. Sea lettuce and dulse should only be picked in winter. Wakame kelp should only be picked during a two-week period. I've never had a bad comment about the flavour of my products. And I cook everything I sell myself. I love to try everything. In ten years of doing this, I've never been to the doctor. I think it helps keep me healthy.

I find that only the adventurous chefs want to buy my products. But those who buy my stuff really want it. The flavours with wild foods can be very intense, so chefs need to experiment and figure out how to use them in moderation. I have long-term relationships with some local chefs. At first they only wanted mushrooms, like chanterelles, but slowly they are experimenting with new types of wild foods. And they say they're getting a positive response from their customers, who want to try local wild foods.

In Nova Scotia, we have lots of potential to sell wild food products to tourists, because they want something that is from here. If they see a bottle of gin that is made with local juniper berries, they want to buy it.

I give educational tours about wild foods, too. We walk and gather foods for two or three hours and then spend an hour in the kitchen cooking and eating with what we collect. It's a lot of fun. During the walks people are amazed at what we have around us. And they realize you don't have to be a great chef to cook with wild foods. Just put a little cream cheese on toast and cover it with flakes of sea lettuce; it's easy and delicious.

Before I came to Canada, I thought that all Canadians would know about the wild foods around them, but most don't. I worry that we, society, are losing our connection to nature, more and more. So I try to help people connect with nature a little bit.

www.fdwildfoods.net

Cloudberry

Chapter 2

Fields, Marshes, Rivers, and Bogs

I f there is a better way to spend an early May morning than ambling through a flood-plain forest, listening to the songs of spring birds and the chatter of a stream, bent low while filling a basket with fiddleheads, I'm in no hurry to find it. An hour or so goes by, my picking partner and I stop to compare our hauls, we share a cup of tea and a sandwich, and we watch the river flow by. For the moment, at least, life is sweet.

Fields, marshes, rivers, and bogs offer a bounty of wild edibles. Look for rich flood-plain forests next to streams and rivers for fiddleheads. Seek out coastal barrens and inland bogs for cranberries, huckleberries, and cloudberries. Look to marshes and the edges of slow rivers for cattails. Fields are the place for blueberries, wild roses, blackberries, stinging nettles, and fireweed. Of course, many plants can grow in a diversity of environments, so keep an eye out wherever you are for a chance encounter with a favourite edible.

Fiddlehead (*Matteuccia struthiopteris*)
a.k.a. Ostrich Fern

For many, fiddleheads top the list of edible wild plants. I start daydreaming about fiddleheads about a month before they emerge. Except for when I was unavoidably out of the country during fiddlehead season, I have enjoyed my annual fiddlehead hunt for some twenty years.

One of my early fiddlehead destinations was the Keswick River in New Brunswick. Friends and I would spend half a day paddling down this small river, stopping frequently to gather bagfuls of fiddleheads. We would enjoy a feast of a picnic on a sandbar and watch the river hurry by, and by end of the day we had more fiddleheads than we knew what to do with. We gave many away, froze some, and ate them three meals a day.

Fiddleheads are the newly emerging and still tightly curled fronds of the ostrich fern. Although the "fiddleheads" of some other ferns are also edible, not all are, so it is important to distinguish the ostrich fern fiddlehead from others. Ostrich fern fiddleheads always grow in clumps, out of a crown that forms the base of the fern. Ostrich fern fiddleheads also have a distinctive U-shaped stem; that is, the stem has a noticeable groove on the inside. Ostrich ferns are found across Canada in every province and territory save for Nunavut. Fiddleheads are one of the few wild edibles that are regularly gathered and sold at farmers' markets and grocery stores.

Fiddleheads grow along rivers that tend to flood in the spring and usually in fairly rich soils that support hardwood trees such as silver maple, red maple, and white ash among others. They often grow with springtime wildflowers such as Dutchman's breeches, wild ginger, and bloodroot, which add beauty for those who take a pause from their picking.

Early to mid-May seems to be the sweet spot for many fiddlehead locations, but the season varies from place to place depending on when the spring flood waters recede. In any event, the picking season usually begins a week or so after the flood waters recede and can last two or three weeks. A friend of mine picked fiddleheads for about a month by following the fiddlehead season on different rivers in New Brunswick. His fingers were dark from the tannins in the fern and cracked and calloused from the long days of picking.

Note: Never pick all of the fiddleheads from one crown. It is critical to leave a few of the fronds (at least half) to ensure the fern survives and the patch remains healthy year after year. I marvel to think that some patches of fiddleheads have been picked by the Mi'kmaq continuously for centuries. Although some people use a knife to sever fiddleheads from their base, I find that fingers work best and avoid the risk of accidentally cutting into and harming the base of the fern.

Do not bring home fiddleheads without washing them in the river first. If you do, you may become so frustrated with trying to clean them in a sink that you will never pick fiddleheads again. Before leaving the river where you pick your fiddleheads, put all of your fiddleheads into some sort of basket with holes. I find that a wicker or plastic laundry hamper works well, provided the holes are small enough to prevent the fiddleheads from floating through. Immerse the basket of fiddleheads in the river and swoosh it slightly. Wait a moment to let the river's current wash away the papery chaff, and repeat until you are left with bright green and clean fiddleheads. It is good to give them another wash at home before cooking but the river rinse should remove almost all the chaff.

For me, fiddleheads are best when boiled in lightly salted water for the perfect amount of time and then served with butter. Sometimes with a bit of salt and touch of lemon juice or vinegar, but nothing more. The perfect amount of time, incidentally, is just after the fiddleheads lose their crunchiness but still remain firm to the tooth, and certainly before they become the slightest bit mushy. Mushy is terrible, crunchy is unpleasant (and may upset your stomach), and the sweet spot is in between. Some people steam fiddleheads but, given the tannins that come out when boiled, I prefer boiling over steaming.

Fiddleheads can be kept in a refrigerator for a week or so in a plastic bag if they are wetted and not dried. I once kept a large quantity of fiddleheads fresh for about ten days by placing them in a canvas bag in a cool stream. To freeze fiddleheads, parboil them first (a couple of minutes in boiling water), then dry them before freezing on a cookie sheet; once frozen, transfer them to sealed containers or bags. Frozen fiddleheads cannot be enjoyed like fresh fiddleheads because freezing seems to destroy their texture and some flavour. However, they are still excellent in soups. When cooking with frozen fiddleheads, add immediately to the pot without thawing first.

Fiddleheads reportedly are strong antioxidants and contain relatively high amounts of potassium, vitamin C, and vitamin A. According to an Agriculture Canada study they are also a source of omega-3 and omega-6 fatty acids, and are high in iron and fibre.

Here's a basic recipe (courtesy of my mother) for creamed fiddlehead soup, which is a good way to use frozen fiddleheads:

Sauté a diced onion in butter until translucent. Add a couple of diced garlic cloves and sauté for another minute or two. Add four or five cups of chicken or vegetable stock to the mix and bring to a boil before adding two cups or so of chopped fresh or frozen fiddleheads, and a couple of chopped carrots and potatoes. Reduce heat and simmer until the vegetables are tender, and then purée with a hand blender to the desired consistency. Stir in two cups of whipping cream (or the heaviest you have on hand) and add salt and pepper to taste. Add more stock to make a thinner soup if desired. You can add tamari and grated cheddar cheese when serving.

Cattail (*Typha angustifolia* and *T. latifolia*)

Cattails grow in marshes and other wet areas, and along the edges of ponds, lakes, and slow-moving rivers. Their tall, thin leaves and brown cattails are unmistakable and characteristic of wet soils that are not too acidic.

I always pull up some of the young cattail shoots when I am picking fiddleheads around mid-May; they often seem to grow somewhere along my path to the fiddleheads. The young cattail shoots can be eaten on the spot, or taken home to be briefly boiled or steamed and eaten with a little butter and salt.

A month or so later in June, the cattail spikes (which are the male flowering structures) can be picked and boiled or steamed for a couple of minutes and then eaten (yes, with a little butter and salt). The spikes are the upper, thinner section of the cattail flowering structure. The time to pick them is when they are first emerging and still wrapped in a green covering. Break the spike off from the thicker lower section (which is the female flowering structure). Yet another food from the cattail is the pollen produced on the male flowers (those you didn't pick and eat). Shake the pollen-laden male flowers into a bag to dislodge the pollen. The pollen can be used in any baking recipe that calls for flour; just substitute a portion of the flour with the cattail pollen. Extra pollen can be frozen for later use.

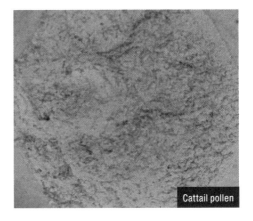

Cattail pollen

Cranberry (*Vaccinium macrocarpon* and *V. oxycoccus*) and Lingonberry (*V. vitis-idaea*) a.k.a. Partridgeberry in Newfoundland & Labrador

Cranberries

Cranberries and lingonberries were staple wild foods for many communities in eastern Canada for generations, and remain so in some places to this day. I remember buying bags of lingonberries in Newfoundland (or partridgeberries, as Newfoundlanders and Labradoreans call them) at farmers' markets and roadside stands, collected by locals from their favourite berry-picking spots.

Cranberries and lingonberries grow in bogs, barrens, along slow-moving rivers, and sometimes at the ocean's edge. In some places they grow in such abundance that a year's supply can be gathered in an afternoon or so. Most people wait until after a frost or two before gathering them.

These berries are, of course, best known for their sauce, which accompanies most Thanksgiving and Christmas meals. The cranberry purchased in stores is *Vaccinium macrocarpon*, the same large cranberry that many people gather in bogs and along the seashore. To make cranberry sauce, simply boil the cranberries with a little water and sugar or other sweetener to taste until most of the berries have popped open, about ten minutes.

Cranberries and lingonberries can also be cooked, mashed, and strained to make juice, or added to muffins and scones. I once took some of my law school classmates picking cranberries so we could make a large batch of cranberry muffins (to fuel our studying, of course). Along the way I showed them juniper berries too and mentioned they can be used as a spice. Later, when eating the first of our cranberry muffins, a jolt of juniper taste exploded in my mouth. Someone had picked a few juniper berries and added them to the bag of cranberries, and we had unknowingly added them to the muffin mix. It was a bit of Russian roulette waiting for the bite of muffin that would give us a lively rush of juniper flavour. We ate them all, though, and almost enjoyed our concoction.

Some favourite treats of mine are the cranberries and lingonberries that can be found as the snow recedes in the spring. Winter transforms the berries into sweet little delights that must be eaten immediately on the spot. Lingonberries reportedly contain a natural preservative, which may explain why they so often survive intact into spring. Lingonberries, by the way, are used in Finland to make a liquor known as lapponia.

Cranberry-Apple Bread

by Frances Buckley, from Newfoundland and Labrador's *Down East Magazine* (October 2011 issue)

1 ½ cups flour
1 ½ teaspoons baking power
1 ½ teaspoons cinnamon
½ teaspoon baking soda
2 cups apples, chopped
¾ cup sugar
2 teaspoons olive oil
1 egg, lightly beaten
1 cup cranberries
½ cup walnuts

Mix flour, baking powder, cinnamon, and baking soda and set aside. Mix apples, sugar, and oil in a bowl. Stir in beaten egg. Add flour mixture, stirring until moistened. Fold in cranberries and walnuts. Batter will be thick—almost more fruit than batter. Transfer batter to a greased loaf pan. Bake at 350° F for 1 hour or until done.

Cranberry

Lingonberry

Huckleberry (*Gaylussacia baccata* and *G. bigeloviana*)

Huckleberry shrubs often grow thickly near bogs and in barrens, and along lake edges and seashores. The berries are ripe in late summer and early fall when they are black, juicy, and sweet.

If you manage to pick some that you do not eat on the spot, bring them home and use them fresh on cereal, porridge, or ice cream. They freeze well and can be used the same way blueberries are, in pies, jams, sauces, or what have you.

Chokeberry (*Aronia* species) looks similar to huckleberry and often grows alongside it. You may pick chokeberry by mistake but you'll know the difference the instant you taste its acerbic flesh. (Don't worry; it's not poisonous and some people eat them for their reported health benefits, and make jam, jelly, wine, and tea from them.) With a bit of practice you can spot chokeberry's finely serrated leaves, which differ from huckleberry's smooth-edged leaves. You may also pick up on the subtle visual differences between the berries themselves.

Huckleberry leaf, left; Aronia leaf, right

In *A Taste of the Wild*, Blanche Garrett recommends making huckleberry bounce: Mash together 2 cups of huckleberries and 3/4 cup of sugar in a large glass jar (Garrett doesn't say how big, but I'm guessing a litre), add 1/8 teaspoon of minced or powdered ginger, fill the jar with brandy and set it aside in a dark place for a couple of months, shaking the jar from time to time. Leave alone for another month if you can, then strain off the brandy to enjoy at your leisure, and eat the huckleberries immediately with ice cream. No huckleberries? Just substitute other berries if you like. I managed to forget about my bottle of huckleberry bounce until Christmas dinner, and served some as a digestif between the turkey and the trifle. All hands pronounced it agreeable and several requested a second round. Its high alcohol content and intense flavour make a little go a long way.

Huckleberry bounce

Blueberry (*Vaccinium angustifolium* and other species)

Photo by Jennifer MacLatchy

There are numerous species of blueberry and all are edible. The lowbush blueberry (*V. angustifolium*) is the most common species that we pick and is also the species that is grown commercially in "wild" blueberry fields.

A handy tool for gathering blueberries is a blueberry rake. Blueberry rakes have wire or wooden tines that comb the bushes and remove the berries. This method also collects a bit of chaff which must be removed either manually or with the help of winnowing. Some people use the blanket method to separate berries from chaff: Place a wide board or table or other flat surface at an angle just steep enough to ensure the berries will roll down it. Cover the surface with a towel or blanket that is fuzzy (a smooth sheet would not work) and slowly pour the blueberries down the incline and collect them in a container at the bottom. The chaff should be left behind on the blanket.

Freezing blueberries in a single layer on a cookie sheet before transferring them to a container helps keep them from freezing together, making it easier to grab a handful of the frozen berries whenever desired.

Blackberry (*Rubus allegheniensis* and other species) and Raspberry (*Rubus idaeus* and *R. pubescens*)

Last summer while I was visiting, my friends' two children took me to a blackberry patch on the edge of an overgrown field near their house. They told me about their various summer adventures while we slowly filled empty yogurt containers, the kids putting at least every other blackberry into their mouths instead of their containers. Focused on my picking I lost sight of the youngest for a while. Then I heard him yelp from inside the blackberry bramble. The eldest and I gingerly pulled the thorny canes away from his arms and legs so he could safely retreat. Blackberry pancakes helped him forget the scratches and tears.

Blackberries and raspberries tend to grow in overgrown fields, at the edges of fields and woods, and alongside roads. They both like full sun if they can get it. Wild patches of these berries can be improved by snipping some of the older canes at their base to encourage the younger, berry-bearing canes, and by cutting pathways through the brambles to create safe passage for foragers.

A close cousin of blackberries and raspberries is the dewberry (*Rubus pubescens*), also known as trailing raspberry or dwarf raspberry. Instead of fields and edges it prefers mixed softwood-hardwood forests, especially those with wet soils, in places where light can reach the forest floor. Rather than support itself on canes like its cousins, dewberries trail along the ground. The berries, though, look very similar to raspberries and taste just as fine.

All of these berries are excellent eaten fresh, of course. They also can be cooked until their juice is released and then strained to remove their seeds. The juice can be used as is, or added to soda water to make a drink, or cooked with sugar to make a syrup, or cooked with sugar and pectin to make jelly.

Heather MacLeod and Barbara MacDonald, authors of *Edible Wild Plants of Nova Scotia*, suggest packing blackberries into a jar and filling the remaining spaces with white vinegar before sealing it and letting sit for a month. Then, strain the juice into sealable sterilized jars for storage. Mix this liquid with soda water or regular water and add a little sugar for a refreshing drink.

As with blueberries, I recommend freezing raspberries and blackberries in a single layer on a cookie sheet first before transferring to a container so that they may be conveniently enjoyed by the handful.

"I love bright red drinks, don't you? They taste twice as good as any other color."
—Lucy Maud Montgomery, *Anne of Green Gables*

Raspberry Cordial, Anne's favourite drink
From *Food & Wine* magazine

2 cups raspberries (1 pint), fresh or frozen
1 tablespoon lemon juice
¾ cup sugar
3 cups water

Add lemon juice to the berries and let sit while you bring the water and sugar to a boil. Pour the boiling water-sugar mix over the berries. Once cool, cover with a tea towel and place in the refrigerator overnight. Strain the mixture through a mesh sieve, pressing a little if you want to extract as much juice as you can (although this may darken the liquid a little). The leftover berry flesh can be added to ice cream or yogurt, and the liquid is stored in the refrigerator. When ready to serve, dilute with water or sparkling water to taste. Add a nip of vodka or gin if you're so inclined.

A Bevy of Tea Plants

Photo by Dan Hutt

Many plants found in fields and at woods' edge can be used for tea, either fresh or dried. Wild strawberry (*Fragaria virginiana*, *F. vesca*) leaves, blackberry leaves, and raspberry leaves can be used on their own or mixed to make a tea. These are all best picked when they are young, before the plants flower. Wild mint (*Mentha* species) is an obvious candidate for tea and can be thrown into a hot bath too to add a little zip to a Sunday evening. The young leaves and flowers of yarrow (*Achillea millefolium*) make an aromatic tea, and stinging nettle (*Urtica dioica*) makes a tea claimed to be healthful. Labrador tea's (*Ledum groenlandicum*) use for hot beverages is self-evident. Clover (*Trifolium* species) flowers make a pleasant tea and are easily dried for winter use.

Whatever the plant, let it steep a few minutes in freshly boiled water. Experiment with amounts and with mixing various plants to make a wild tea blend. According to Anne Gardon, author of *The Wild Food Gourmet*, coureurs de bois enjoyed a blend of one-third each of Labrador tea, wintergreen, and conifer tree twigs.

Sweet fern (*Comptonia peregrina*) can be made into a sun tea by letting a handful of its leaves sit in a bottle of water in the sun for several hours. This is a good use for mint as well.

Cloudberry

Cloudberry (*Rubus chamaemorus*)
a.k.a. Bakeapple (or Baie Qu'appelle)

Photo by Dan Hutt

Photo by Dan Hutt

If you know of a cloudberry patch in the Maritimes, I would understand if you chose not to divulge its location until you were on your deathbed. While fairly common in Newfoundland and Labrador, cloudberries are a precious find anywhere in the Maritimes. I happened upon a large patch once on an undisclosed island along Nova Scotia's Atlantic coast. My partner and I had kayaked there and walked into the interior of the island to stretch our legs. My jaw dropped at the sight of a large field of the golden-yellow berries. I find cloudberries addictive and could not stop picking and eating until I had scoured that field in search of the last ripe berry. If I had more restraint I would collect enough for cloudberry jam.

I will leave the discussion of cloudberries at that. Perhaps I have said too much already, and ought to have simply lied and said that they do not grow in the Maritimes.

Dandelion (*Taraxacum officinale*)

A friend of mine once told me a story of how as a child she and her first-generation American-Italian family picked apples in U-pick orchards. Her great-aunt, barely four feet high, couldn't reach the apples so contented herself with picking dandelion greens. When paying for the apples they always asked whether they needed to weigh the greens as well, to which the orchard managers always replied, "Nope, the weeds are free." My friend is now a consummate forager herself and treasures the memories of her great-aunt energetically picking dandelion greens for her minestra (a dandelion and pepperoni soup) and other traditional dishes. See my friend's family recipe for minestra soup on page 77.

I remember Hal Hinds, author of *Flora of New Brunswick*, telling me with a gleam in his eye about his passion for devouring quantities of dandelion greens in the spring. I too have a springtime hunger for dandelion greens and my mouth waters just thinking about them. Dandelion greens contain lots of vitamin A and C and other minerals and nutrients (riboflavin, thiamine, calcium, sodium, and potassium), which perhaps is why those who eat them tend to crave them come spring.

The trick with dandelions is to get them before they flower. Although bitter enough before they flower, they become nearly inedible after flowering. If you miss the spring flush of greens before the yellow flowers appear, wait for the second round of young dandelions in late August. You can continue to pick them into the fall as these summer-germinated plants grow.

I like to pick the crown of the dandelion plant. That is, I like to get the whole plant just above the root with leaves still attached and perhaps the little flower buds nestled at the base of the leaves (but not extended on a stalk).

If you are lucky enough to have dandelions in your garden, dig them up roots and all and soak them whole in a bucket of water before scrubbing the dirt from the roots. Cook the whole plant in boiling water until the leaves turn bright green. Drain the water, cut the roots from the upper portion of the plant, and put the roots back in the pot with fresh water to simmer for another five or ten minutes. Meanwhile, melt a little butter into the greens, add a pinch of salt and squeeze of lemon, and enjoy one of the best springtime meals going. When you've finished eating the greens, drain the water from the roots, add butter, salt, and lemon to them, and enjoy your second course.

The youngest dandelion leaves can also be eaten raw, either mixed with a salad or on their own with a vinaigrette dressing or olive oil, lemon juice, and salt. If you pick the leaves a bit too late and find them too bitter, try boiling them in two changes of water to make them more palatable. Adding a dash of baking soda to the water can help as well.

You can roast dandelion roots in an oven until they are dry enough to snap when bent. They smell remarkably good while roasting and you may be tempted to eat some of them once toasted—don't hold back. Take those you don't snack on and snap them into bits or use a food grinder or processor to chop them up and then steep them in freshly boiled water to make a hot beverage. Some sources describe this dandelion root beverage as a substitute for coffee. Nonsense. If you want coffee, drink coffee. Dandelion root is its own delightful drink. A little milk and honey can complement it nicely. I am not sure I would ever attempt this, but for daring souls here's a dandelion wine recipe as recorded by Heather MacLeod and Barbara MacDonald in *Edible Wild Plants of Nova Scotia*.

Pick a gallon of dandelion flowers. Pour a gallon of boiling water over the petals and let sit covered for ten days, stirring occasionally. Strain the liquid to remove the flowers, put the liquid into a pot with four pounds of sugar, one orange, and one lemon sliced thinly, and boil for twenty minutes. Make a piece of toast, spread a cake of yeast on the toast, and add the toast to the liquid once it has cooled to a warm but not scalding temperature. Cover and leave for two days, then strain the liquid into a five-gallon carboy (a glass container used by wine and beer makers), cork with an airlock cork (this can be purchased from a wine and beer making store), and let ferment for two months before bottling.
If you try this and the result is drinkable, please invite me over to taste some.

Dandelions can be grown indoors in the winter. Simply dig up some dandelion plants in the fall, plant them in a container of soil or sand, cover with plastic to keep them moist, and store in a cool dark place such as a cold basement or garage. Sometime during the winter, uncover them and bring them into a warmer location in the house and you'll soon be enjoying the tender new growth.

My Mama's Dandelion Soup (Minestra)
Courtesy of Maria Recchia, Bocabec, New Brunswick (who mentioned that her family never measured anything when cooking)

Olive oil
Garlic
Pepperoni
Dandelion greens
Canned cannellini beans (a.k.a. white kidney beans)

Wash dandelion greens well, chop into two-inch-long pieces, and sit in a bowl of water.

Heat olive oil, minced garlic, and diced pepperoni over low heat until garlic is soft but not browned. Add the dandelion greens with the water that clings to them. Cover and cook over high heat until greens are very tender. Add canned beans with liquid.

Continue to cook until heated through. Salt to taste. Best if allowed to sit for thirty minutes or more before serving. Serve with grated parmesan or pecorino romano cheese and crusty French or Italian bread.

Japanese Knotweed (*Reynoutria japonica* var. *japonica*) a.k.a. Mexican Bamboo

Native to eastern Asia, Japanese knotweed was introduced to the United States in the late 1800s as an ornamental and erosion-control plant and was judged an immediate success. Too successful, it turned out. The plant can spread along roadsides and riverbanks, and displace native vegetation wherever it takes root. It makes the top-one hundred list of the world's most invasive species.

A member of the buckwheat family, Japanese knotweed has hollow, smooth, jointed stems. Purplish when the stalks first emerge in early spring, they eventually turn green with red flecks. They grow astonishingly quickly, shooting up as much as eight centimetres a day and reaching a height of one to three metres over the course of the summer. The stems die back to the ground in fall, only to sprout up the following spring.

No one wants a patch of this plant on their property. If you do have this plant, you might want to research ways to eradicate it before it spreads any further. However, this is a book on wild edibles, so while you're eradicating this noisome plant, why not snack on it too?

Photo by Jakob Lutes

In early spring before their leaves unfurl, the young shoots, up to a foot or so high, can be eaten raw or cooked with a little sugar to make a dessert. In terms of the taste, think of them as rhubarb-lite (cooked Japanese knotweed looks something like stewed rhubarb too). I've turned the shoots into a sweet sauce for yogurt and ice cream, and have made a pleasant knotweed-ginger jam. For jam, just cook them with enough sugar to make them sweet, add ginger to the mix, and then bottle. Some lemon juice might be worth adding too. Before cooking, cut the stalks into short rounds to avoid having long sections of stringy fibres in the sauce. The stalks can also be simply boiled in a little salted water to make a savoury side dish.

Stinging Nettle (*Urtica dioica*)

I seem to find stinging nettle almost exclusively around old farmhouses or homesteads. Look for its saw-tooth-like leaves, its hanging clusters of tiny green flowers, and its steep upside-down cone-shape appearance. They often grow in full sunlight in large groups, usually to a height of a metre or so.

As the name suggests, this plant packs a punch if you brush up against it with unprotected skin. I became acutely aware of this defence mechanism when doing botanical surveys along the St. John River, once upon a time. It's not pleasant. Needless to say, make sure to wear gloves, pants, and a long-sleeved shirt when collecting stinging nettle. If you do get a dose of this plant's venom (formic acid), wash the area with water (and soap if you have it) and put something cool and moist on it. If there is jewelweed (*Impatiens pallida* or *I. capensis*) nearby, try squeezing a bit of juice from its stem onto the affected area.

Believe it or not, nettle is worth the safety preparations required to collect it. Boiling or drying rids the plant of its sting, and once declawed the plant makes a tasty, spinach-like green. Dried nettle is commonly used to make tea (reportedly rich in iron). Tea is also sometimes made from the roots of the plant and is said to have medicinal properties. To make nettle tea, pour freshly boiled water over leaves (fresh or dried) and let sit for a few minutes.

For a feed of nettle greens, collect the stems and leaves in spring to early summer and boil, steam, or sauté them for a few minutes until tender. Serve with (you guessed it) a little butter and salt. Make a soup out of the fresh leaves and stems or add them to a pasta dish.

Wild Rose (*Rosa virginiana*, *Rosa rugosa*, and others)

Many old fields, roadsides, and seashores are brightened with the pink petals and red hips of wild roses. True wild roses are mostly *Rosa virginiana*, although there are other wild roses native to eastern Canada as well. Along with these are cultivars that have gone rogue from gardens and homesteads, in places naturalizing themselves alongside their wild cousins. *Rosa rugosa*, or beach rose, is a common non-native species growing along our coastlines, considered to be an invasive species by some.

Heart-shaped rose petals can be plucked and placed upon your tongue as you take a slow summer's walk along the seashore. Or collect a handful to colour a salad. Rosehips can be nibbled from fall through winter. I picked them often as a kid during winter walks and carefully ate the frozen red skin and orange flesh away from the inner seeds, which are disagreeable and best discarded. Eaten fresh, rosehips are rich in vitamin C.

Both petals and hips can be dried for making tea. Before drying the hips, cut them in half and remove the seedy core. Both can also be used for jelly and jam. For petal jam, gather about two cups' worth of petals and bring to a boil in about a cup and a half of water. Add one to two cups of sugar, three tablespoons of lemon juice, and 3/4 tablespoon of pectin, then simmer for twenty minutes or so. Keep the jam in the refrigerator or place into sterilized jars.

For rosehip jelly, chop six cups of rosehips and simmer them for an hour in two cups of water. Strain them through cheese cloth and add about four cups of sugar to the strained liquid. Bring to a boil, stirring, and add pectin. Boil another five minutes, stirring often, then place into sterilized jars.

For a rosehip purée dessert, boil about two cups of rosehips until soft and then press through a sieve to remove the seeds and skins. Add a cup of water and two tablespoons of sugar to the resulting purée and bring back to a boil, stirring constantly. Let cool and then place in the refrigerator. Add whipped cream on top when serving.

Jerusalem Artichoke (*Helianthus tuberosus*)
a.k.a. Sunchokes

Jerusalem artichokes are a sunflower that grows edible underground tubers. Is it native to eastern Canada? Some say yes, some say no. It's possible that Indigenous people introduced them to the region centuries ago.

To find them just dig a little around the plants in the fall or even in the winter so long as the ground isn't too frozen. They seem to grow along rivers and in old fields, and some people plant them for the tubers or sometimes just for the fall flowers. You might find the tubers for sale at farmers' markets. Jerusalem artichokes are easy to grow on one's own property—sometimes too easy. They can readily take over an area if not kept in check and shouldn't be planted in a vegetable garden.

The tubers can be eaten raw (grated or sliced thinly works well) or boiled or roasted like potatoes. Here's a recipe for Jerusalem artichoke soup, provided by the Ecology Action Centre's *Adventures in Local Food* blog:

Cream of Jerusalem Artichoke Soup
(Serves 6–8 people)

2 pounds (1kg) Jerusalem artichokes, well-scrubbed
1 tablespoon (15 mL) butter
1 large cooking onion, chopped
1/2 pound (250g) celery root, peeled and chopped
6 cups (1.5L) homemade stock (we used homemade veggie stock)
1 cup heavy cream (we used cream blend)
salt, pepper (white pepper preferably), and lemon juice to taste
top with fresh parsley

Chop the Jerusalem artichokes and place them in a bowl of cold water to prevent blackening. In a large saucepan, melt butter over medium heat. Gently sauté onion and celery root until soft, about five minutes. Add Jerusalem artichokes and stock. Simmer twenty minutes or until tender. Purée with a hand blender, and whisk in cream.

Coltsfoot (*Tussilago farfara*)

Photo by Creative Commons

Coltsfoot flowers **appear before** their leaves grow and even before dandelions bloom. Coltsfoot leaves don't show up until after the flowers have finished blooming, which might lead some to think of them as two separate plants. To find the flowering stocks simply look for the yellow, low-growing leafless flowers along roadsides in early spring. Coltsfoot was introduced from Europe many years ago, perhaps even purposely by early colonialists for use as a medicinal plant or food. Its Latin name refers to its traditional use to treat coughs and sore throats. An old name for the plant is coughwort.

Importantly, the plant contains toxic alkaloids that can cause medical problems if consumed in large quantities. Pregnant women should avoid coltsfoot and infants should not be given coltsfoot.

To prepare, pick young stems when their flowers are just opened or about to open and boil or stir-fry. What do they taste like? Somewhere between broccoli, asparagus, and fiddleheads, I thought when I first tried them. In other words, pretty darn good.

Lambs Quarters *(Chenopodium album)*

Photo by Bernell MacDonald

Lambs quarters is a cousin to spinach and beets and is a common weed in gardens and farm fields. I sometimes let these weeds grow a little in my garden before yanking them for a bonus harvest. I've found copious amounts of healthy, vibrant lambs quarters growing on a friend's old manure pile. They also seem to be quite common along some shorelines. I gathered lots of lambs quarters when I was a kid from the shoreline in my hometown of St. Andrews, New Brunswick.

They are high in vitamin C and iron and can be eaten raw in salads or cooked as a green—boiled, steamed, or stir-fried—just like spinach. I find they have a better texture and flavour than spinach when cooked, and find too that my body craves a meal of them in spring.

Groundnut (*Apios americana*)
a.k.a. Apios, Hopniss, Wild Bean

Photo by Alain Belliveau

Groundnut was once upon a time a staple for those Indigeous people who overlapped with its distribution. And groundnut is another food that reportedly saved the Pilgrims from starving. Nutritious and plentiful, the potato-like tubers that grow along the plant's roots range from dime- to egg-size and even larger. A member of the pea family—a legume—*apios* also has edible beans growing in long pods that look similar to garden green beans. Its blue to pink flower clusters, growing along the length of its vine-like, snaking stem, are reminiscent of those of black locust (another legume, incidentally).

The beans can be shelled from their pods and eaten after a brief boiling. But the main event is the protein-rich tubers, which can be baked or sliced and fried with butter and salt. The tubers are a little sweet and a little nutty, and are best collected in late autumn or early spring when they are at their sweetest.

Groundnuts tend to grow on lake edges and riverbanks, especially those with rich soils. To harvest the tubers, follow a vine back to the ground and start digging. Since groundnuts are better in the late fall, you may find that the above-ground portion of the plant has already withered away by the time you're ready to harvest. It's not a bad idea to identify a good patch of groundnut during the summer to make it easier to find come fall. Otherwise, try to find the dried groundnut vine and then follow it back to its source. If you collect more than you can use right away, store the excess in a root cellar if you have one.

"With my eyes shut I should not have known but I was eating a somewhat soggy potato." —Henry David Thoreau on eating groundnuts for the first time. Perhaps he should have sautéed them!

Plantain (*Plantago major*)
a.k.a. Broadleaf Plantain

An unassuming plant that grows in backyards and dooryards and alongside streets and sidewalks, you've likely trodden upon the lowly plantain more than once. Often keeping company with blades of grass and dandelion flowers, it has an impressive ability to grow in compacted soil and other challenging urban and disturbed areas. Its fleshy, rounded-oval leaves are best eaten when they first appear in the spring and they are most tender, but can be eaten into the fall. Although they can be eaten raw, they improve with boiling or steaming and a little butter and salt. Unfortunately, older plantain leaves have tough, stringy fibres that are best removed before eating, which can be done by pulling them through your teeth if you and your company aren't too fussy.

Whether by accident or perhaps on purpose, plantain was one of the first plants to find its way from Europe to North America. The plant has long been valued both as a food and as a medicinal herb and received at least two mentions by Shakespeare. Costard, in *Love's Labour's Lost*, exclaims: "O, sir, plantain, a plain plantain!" (For his cut shin.) And in *Romeo and Juliet*, Romeo quips to Benvolio that "Your plantain leaf is excellent for that." "For what, I pray thee?" Benvolio responds. "For your broken [cut] shin," replies Romeo, perhaps comparing Benvolio's remedy for lovesickness to a mere band-aid treatment.

Grape (*Vitis riparia* and others)
a.k.a. Riverbank Grape

Stumbling across wild-growing grapes for the first time was a pleasant shock. I hadn't imagined that grapes—small and sour, yes, but grapes nonetheless—were native to eastern Canada. I hadn't imagined that grapes were anything but the cultivated ones found in grocery stores. My companion and I filled a backpack with the intense purple fruit, thrilled with visions of jars full of jelly.

Although the story is debated, Norse explorers may also have stumbled across these juicy berries more than a thousand years ago in what is now northern New Brunswick, during their far-ranging ocean voyages. They called their discovery Vinland, perhaps in honour of grapes they found growing there. An archaeological dig at a Viking settlement in Newfoundland found nuts from butternut trees, which grow only as far north as New Brunswick, suggesting that Leif Eiríksson and his Viking crew sailed at least that far south and west.

The wild riverbank grape is native only as far east as New Brunswick, growing along the banks of the St. John River and other waterways with rich flood-plain soils. However, it can also be found either planted or escaped occasionally throughout the rest of the Maritimes. Various cultivated varieties of grapes can be found when exploring old homesteads where the old homes have long since disappeared, leaving behind a stone foundation, some lilacs, and perhaps a surviving hop or grape vine. I've been lucky to find hops and grapes and even currants near old homestead sites, and I wonder about the people who lived there as I benefit from their long-ago labours.

What to do with grapes? First thing is to leave them on the vine until a frost has touched them in order to get them at their least tart. Grapes do not ripen once picked, so it's crucial not to pick them too soon. Then, eat them if you have a taste for them. Some swallow the seeds whole; others enjoy crunching them. Jelly is a good use for grapes. Cook them until they are easily mashed and then strain the liquid from the seeds and skins. Add lots of sugar and enough pectin so that a spoonful of the hot liquid sets when put on a plate in the freezer for a moment. Pour hot into sterilized jars.

Live-forever (*Hylotelephium telephium*)
a.k.a. Orpine, Garden Stonecrop, Sedum

Photo by Jakob Lutes

Native to Europe, live-forever is a fleshy-leaved (succulent) plant likely brought across the Atlantic Ocean as a garden flower, perhaps as a reminder of home by some early colonist. Or perhaps it was packed across the ocean for its culinary value. In any event, live-forever adapted well to its new home, soon bidding adieu to its garden confines and spreading into overgrown fields and wild woods, thriving in slightly shady environments and rich soils.

Live-forever dies back in the winter and perennially grows up from the same roots each spring. Live-forever is one of the earliest plants to send up shoots and their small rosettes of vibrant green-cupped leaves contrast with surrounding winter-dead grass and fallen leaves. It can reach about half a metre high by early summer, but it is the young, tender, mild-flavoured springtime shoots that you want for your salad or for nibbling as you walk. Live-forever can also be added to stir-fries or steamed or boiled as a cooked green. Outside of its springtime tenderness, live-forever is best cooked.

If in need of a diversion, pluck a mature, fleshy leaf of live-forever and gently rub it between your thumb and forefinger. Once you feel the top layer of the leaf separate from the lower, gently blow into the base of the leaf. With practice, you will soon be creating little leaf balloons, reminiscent of a frog's belly. Moreover, you will be a hero to all children present.

You may be a little confused by live-forever's scientific name, and rightly so. Live-forever is also known by many as sedum, and indeed live-forever once belonged to the *Sedum* genus of plants. Discerning botanists, however, decided to shake things up a little and moved live-forever into the *Hylotelephium* genus. Many people, of course, still know this plant as sedum, botanists be damned.

**An interview with Chef Jakob Lutes,
Port City Royal, Saint John,
New Brunswick**

I paused a moment when I first stepped into Jakob Lutes's Port City Royal restaurant, in Saint John, New Brunswick. The gorgeous bar, the bare brick walls, the *Easy Rider* movie still, the massive black leather couch: I had to take in the rich atmosphere before I could even think about looking at the menu. Jakob's passion is drawing flavour from local ingredients combined into small batches of traditional dishes. His dedication has paid off: Port City Royal was recognized as one of the best new restaurants in Canada in 2015 by e*nRoute* magazine. When he can, Jakob adds the wild foods that he collects on foraging expeditions into his dishes.

I actually have a limited knowledge about foraging. I know a few plants well, which I collect, but I'm envious of talented foragers.

It started with my grandmother. She didn't call it foraging, but that's what she did. I remember her collecting goose tongue greens, for example, and blueberries and cranberries. I especially remember her freshly picked blueberries. Funny, I didn't like the goose tongue greens as a kid, but now I crave them. I usually forage with my restaurant manager, Eric Scouten, and he also remembers his family foraging for various wild foods when he was a kid.

I started getting interested in foraging before I became a chef. Now, as a chef, I'm always looking for new flavours so foraging for wild foods makes sense. Eric and I collect and serve quite a few different wild plants, such as coltsfoot, knotweed, fiddleheads, white pine needles, sedum, yarrow, vetch flowers, rose petals, beach peas, pineapple weed, oh and of course goose tongue. If it's got a good, interesting flavour, then I like to use it.

And I love the challenge of cooking with wild foods. I mean, no textbook will tell you how to use yarrow flavour, so it's an adventure. I add yarrow to a potato dish by infusing cream with yarrow before adding it to the potatoes and serving it with salt cod. I also make a spice mix that includes yarrow. I get a good reaction from my customers. Actually, I'm not sure they know they're eating wild foods; they just eat it and love it.

Finding or sourcing enough wild foods for the restaurant can be difficult for us, so wild foods are often just additions to meals rather than the main course. Plus, I'm careful not to deplete any one source, so I usually take small amounts. But that's okay because with wild plants, often a little goes a long way in giving flavour to a dish.

Part of why I love foraging so much is it gets me out to beautiful places. I've seen more of New Brunswick this past couple of years than the rest of my life.

Sedum (live-forever) and arugula salad with grilled onion vinaigrette

4 onions
10 grams garlic
500 grams apple cider vinegar
250 grams sugar
200 grams grainy mustard of your choice
2 grams black pepper
15 grams Worcestershire sauce
50 grams olive oil
100 grams canola oil

Cut the onions in half. Cover the cut surface in oil and grill until cooked, dark brown, and beginning to char. Remove from the grill. When the onions are cool, discard the skins, then place into a food processor with the garlic, cider, sugar, mustard, pepper, and Worcestershire sauce. With the processor running, slowly add the oil to emulsify. Season to taste.

Serve the onion vinaigrette with fresh sedum, dandelion, chive, and anything else that grows in the early spring.

Contributed by Jacob Lutes

Juniper berries and sea urchin

Chapter 3

Seashore and Intertidal Areas

Part 1: Seaside Plants

Goose Tongue
Sea-Rocket
Beach Pea
Sea Spinach
Crowberry
Juniper
Bayberry
Sea Blite
Glasswort
Scotch Lovage
An Interview with Bryan Picard, The Bite House

My first foraging was along the beach in my hometown of St. Andrews, New Brunswick. Someone had given me a book called *Lobster Pots and Searocket Sandwiches* when I was about ten years old. It was written for young people, I think, and each page was playfully illustrated with a family of cartoon hedgehogs going about various adventures in search of seashore edibles. I spent many hours exploring the shoreline and gradually learning the various plants and shellfish described in the book's pages. I still have it on my bookshelf, all these years later.

If for some reason I ever had to survive on wild edibles (pray that never comes to pass), I would hope to find myself near the seashore. With its abundance of easily gathered edible plants and animals, one just might stave off starvation a while on the seashore. Eastern Canada's shorelines are diverse. From rocky headlands with no beaches, to saltwater marshes, to near endless tidal mud flats, each section of coast has its own complement of wild foods. Berries (cranberries, lingonberries, juniper berries, and crowberries) are often found on rocky headlands. Glasswort and sea blite are usually found on sandy or silty beaches at or below the high-tide mark. Orach, beach peas, lambs quarters, and sea-rocket are found just above the high-tide mark on gravel and sand beaches. Edible seaweeds are found on various types of coastline, either washed up on the beach following a storm or picked from their particular section of the seafloor (some above the low-water mark and some below). Soft-shell clams are found in a wide range of substrates, from mud to near gravel. Razor clams, however, only live in the softest and finest substrates. Quahogs are found only below the low-tide mark, necessitating a walk in the water.

The seashore is an attractive area for foraging because it also offers some of the few foods that can be collected during the winter. Once in a while a beach will freeze nearly solid making it impossible to dig for clams, but that is a rare day and likely getting rarer. I have a Christmas tradition of digging a few feeds of clams from a beach within walking distance of the home of some good friends. My friends' children adore clams and we feast on them together. They are almost old enough now to help dig the clams as well as eat them. They love the muddy treasure hunt even if they don't yet add many to the bucket.

Goose Tongue (*Plantago maritima*)
a.k.a. Seaside Plantain

Goose tongue is a seaside species of plantain found along much of eastern Canada's shoreline. It grows in clusters of sharp narrow leaves and is one of the first greens that can be collected along the seashore in the spring. I assume they resemble goose tongues, but I haven't yet bothered to find a goose for comparison.

I have enjoyed goose tongue a good number of times, so was perplexed when I cooked up a batch that I eventually tossed into the compost. Bitter and tough. Then I happened upon someone's story of a similar experience. As it turns out, goose tongue that grows out of rocky crevices on exposed shorelines may be less palatable than goose tongue found growing in more amiable conditions.

At any rate, for a nice side dish of goose tongue just steam or boil for about ten minutes and serve with butter.

Sea-Rocket (*Cakile edentula*)

I think sea-rocket was the first spicy food I ever ate as a child. "Try this!" I'd say to friends, eager to see their reaction. A member of the mustard family, sea-rocket's fleshy leaves can be nibbled raw or added to salads for a little zip. Same with the green seedpods. Once dry, the seeds resemble mustard seeds and can be substituted for them.

Add the leaves to a Montreal-style smoked-meat sandwich or cook them, stems included, for a nice side dish (and for less spicy heat). I haven't tried it yet, but I imagine I could substitute sea-rocket for wasabi in homemade sushi.

Beach Pea (*Lathyrus japonicus*)

Once, while camping on the Maine coast, a friend and I got caught without much food for a proper supper and all the nearby stores and restaurants had closed for the day. We had with us a bit of dry pasta and olive oil. We went to work collecting the young flower buds of beach peas and soon had enough, cooked in seawater and combined with the pasta, to keep our bellies content and our good mood preserved.

Beach peas are just that: peas growing on the beach. Smaller than their garden cousins, they can be eaten in the same way. Add the young pods to a stir-fry. Open the ripe pods and snack on the sweet, miniature peas... if you can get them before they mature into hardened seeds. The withered pods can be opened to collect dried peas that you can add to soups (or just boil into a pea mush, I imagine). In late spring and early summer the flower buds can be picked and eaten raw, or better yet boiled for a few minutes and served with a little butter.

Note, there are some reports that eating large quantities (that is, composing more than a third of one's diet for an extended period of time) of beach peas (that is, the seeds) can lead to a serious disease known as lathyrism. All sources I have reviewed, however, note that the peas are safe when eaten in moderate amounts.

Sea Spinach (*Atriplex* species)
a.k.a. Orach, Orache, Saltbush

A relative of spinach, the young, tender sea spinach leaves can be eaten raw or its leaves and stems can be boiled or steamed. It's an easy side dish to prepare when camping on the coast. Sea spinach sometimes grows near lambs quarters and the two can be cooked together. Try substituting sea spinach or lambs quarters in a spinach soup recipe.

Crowberry (*Empetrum nigrum*)
a.k.a. Mossberry

I cannot help but pick a few handfuls of these enticingly plump, black-skinned little berries whenever I see them, but I quickly find I've had enough before I get many into me. Yet, I always eventually go back for more.

Empetrum means "growing on rocks" and that's what these tenacious plants do. Low to the ground, they often carpet coastal areas that would otherwise be nearly barren. Crowberries can be found along most any exposed rocky shoreline in eastern Canada. I've yet to try cooking with them but I think they would be good cooked with a little sugar to make a sauce for ice cream or yogurt. Some people make jam and jelly with them. They are reportedly high in vitamins C and K. Because many crowberries survive the winter still attached to the plant, they can be picked in early spring as the snow recedes.

Juniper (*Juniperus communis*)

Juniper is another tenacious plant often found along our coastlines and in bogs and barrens. It is a woody shrub that sensibly creeps along the ground rather than stand up to be pummelled by coastal winds. Juniper's needles are prickly and its small, hard berries are green at first but turn blue as they mature over the span of a couple of years' time. It is the bluish berries that are usually collected for cooking.

Juniper berries are best used as a spice for meat or chicken dishes. As previously mentioned I once accidentally mixed a few juniper berries into a batch of cranberry muffins, and although interesting I wouldn't recommend it. My botany professor at Acadia University once explained how to make something resembling gin with laboratory alcohol and juniper berries. I wouldn't recommend that either. Gin is, of course, flavoured with juniper berries, although through a more refined method than that described by my professor.

Juniper berries can be picked and simply stored in a jar without need to refrigerate or freeze. The bluish berries will darken as they dry but that's no matter for concern. Fresh or dry the berries can be crushed and added to marinades or simply rubbed onto the surface of a roast. A teaspoon to a tablespoon is plenty for most dishes—don't overdo it. Germans sometimes flavour sauerkraut with the berries and I like to season roasts of chicken and lamb with them. Experiment a little and treat your dinner guests to a taste that can come only from a prickly, tenacious, salt-sprayed, ocean-side evergreen.

Bayberry (*Morella pensylvanica*)
a.k.a. Wax-myrtle, Candleberry

This fragrant seaside shrub produces clusters of wax-covered grey berries (or drupes, technically). Whenever I walk by bayberry I can't help brushing my hands through its leaves to release a little of its scent. Bayberry, incidentally, is one of a select group of plants that have a symbiotic relationship with a certain type of bacteria that takes nitrogen from the air and converts it to a form usable by plants. It's for this reason that bayberry thrives in marginal, nutrient-poor soils.

Bayberry's drupes are gathered not for eating but rather for their wax. Easily gathered, the drupes are heated in water until their wax melts off and the remaining seed sinks to the bottom. Try not to let the water boil, in order to retain more of the bayberry fragrance. Once the wax has melted from the drupes, let the water cool and the scented bayberry wax will solidify on the surface of the water. Use it to make bayberry candles or add it to homemade soap recipes. If making candles consider adding some beeswax to the mix (up to one part beeswax to two parts bayberry wax).

Don't use your best pots for making wax—you risk the wrath of your house companion. Rubbing alcohol can be used to remove wax from pots, though, should the need arise. Here's a recipe for bayberry soap, from *Lobster Pots and Searocket Sandwiches*:

Dissolve two tablespoons of lye in one-third cup of cold water. Use enamel or iron utensils. Do not use aluminum. The lye will heat up the water. Wait for the container to cool to lukewarm. Never test the liquid with your fingers. Next pour the lye solution into one cup of melted wax. Stir slowly for 15–20 minutes. Pour into molds and keep in a warm place for three days. For molds you can use a flat enamel pan.

Bayberry's shiny leaves can be steeped to make a relaxing tea or substituted for bay leaves in stews and soups. Like bay leaves bought in the supermarket, bayberry leaves can be dried until brittle and stored for winter-long use as a reminder of warmer days.

   A bayberry candle burnt to the socket
   Brings luck to the house and gold to the pocket.
   – Version of an early American colonist saying

Sea Blite (*Suaeda maritima* and other species)

Sea blite is one of those few flowering plants that can live below the high-tide mark. These plants are often completely covered with seawater for a portion of each day. Thanks to this saltwater home sea blite is naturally salty, so when cooked no salt need be added. Sea blite is common in salt marshes and other areas with muddy intertidal zones.

The whole plant is edible either raw or cooked for about five minutes. Collect from spring through to early fall.

Glasswort (*Salicornia* species)
a.k.a. Glassworth, Samphire, Pickleweed

This leafless plant with succulent, branching, almost translucent stems growing near the high-tide mark looks like no other. Green in spring and summer and turning reddish in part or whole in the fall, glasswort usually grows in salt marshes and other tidal areas.

Glasswort can be snacked on raw but is excellent when boiled, steamed, or sautéed for five minutes or so. As with sea blite, glasswort comes with its own sea salt. The topmost portion of the plant is the tenderest. The lower parts can be eaten too, provided you pull out an inner fibrous core after cooking.

As one of its common names suggests, glasswort was once commonly pickled. Here's one way: If using the lower portion of the plant, cook lightly first to enable removal of the fibrous centre. If using the upper, tender parts, there's no need to cook. Put a little mustard seed and peppercorns into each Mason jar (sterilized first) and then pack in the glasswort. Add fresh dill or dill seeds and garlic and chili peppers if you like. Bring equal parts water and white vinegar to a boil then pour over the glasswort, being sure to leave a little air space at the top of each jar (about half an inch or one centimetre). Where's the salt? Glasswort brings its own salt to the party. Remember to cut the glasswort in lengths short enough to be fully submerged in the jars. If you intend to store your pickles without refrigeration, it's a good idea to boil the packed jars (with lids just loosely on) for ten minutes. Let them stew in their jars for a few weeks before digging in.

For a sweet pickle, add sugar to the water and vinegar mix. Euell Gibbons, of *Stalking the Blue-Eyed Scallop* fame, adds a twist by adding a few bayberry leaves to his glasswort pickle.

Scotch Lovage (*Ligusticum scoticum*)
a.k.a. Sea Lovage, Scottish Licorice Root

Scotch lovage is a plant that seems to unassumingly appear most anywhere along the coast. Any number of times I've paused during a seacoast hike and after a moment or two noticed the lovage, there by my feet. I say hello, tear a bit of lovage leaf to nibble, and continue on.

Tolerant of salt spray, scotch lovage makes its home along our rocky shores. It usually grows in dense clumps here and there and its shiny, three-lobed leaves are hard to miss. They resemble a larger, heartier version of celery leaves.

Like many plants, scotch lovage stems and leaves are most tender when they first show themselves in the spring. Nonetheless, the whole plant can be picked at any time. The leaves can be cooked as a green or added to soups or stews. The taste resembles celery with an extra kick. Remember to pick enough for friends, so you can—wait for it— spread the lovage.

The celery taste is no accident. Scotch lovage, along with garden-variety lovage, belongs to the Umbelliferae family (also known as the Apiaceae family), along with celery, parsley, carrots, parsnips, and…oh the list is long. The family is so named for their umbel-shaped flower clusters. What's an umbel? Think umbrella.

With permission of the landowner, you can dig up a scotch lovage plant to transplant to your garden. Or collect a few seeds for the same purpose. The seeds have the same lovage taste as the leaves and are easily saved through the winter. Just collect a bunch, make sure they're dry, and put them in a jar in your spice cupboard.

An Interview with Bryan Picard, The Bite House

Chef Bryan Picard operates a small restaurant near Baddeck, Cape Breton. Want to try one of his elaborate meals? It's wise to make your reservation well in advance; the Bite House is often booked up.

The thing with wild foods is that the season is so short. A lot of things last only a few weeks, or less. But that means there's always something different. I think I have something like twenty wild edibles close to where I live, so there's almost always something to pick.

The seashore is also a favourite place of mine to forage. Sea asparagus, or glasswort some people call it, is a favourite, a nice salty succulent. I like it raw or sautéed just a little. I do a lot with making my own herbs and spices using wild foods. I dry pineapple weed and crumble it onto desserts. I dry spruce tips too, and then powder them so I can add to different dishes. I've put dried spruce tips in my smoker too, to give them a nice smoky flavour. I like making apple blossom vinegar, or even adding fresh apple blossoms to a dish as a garnish.

Every year I find a few new spots for one thing or another, and I add to my list of places to forage for a particular food. A friend just told me about a good spot for stinging nettles. Foraging does take a lot of time, but it's good to get outside and enjoy the fresh air. And my dad has really gotten into foraging, so he's been collecting a lot for the restaurant.

People usually know about wild mushrooms, but there's so much more out there than just mushrooms. Sometimes my customers are a little afraid to try new things, but I just let them know how delicious these foods can be.

thebitehouse.com

Part 2: Seaweeds, a.k.a. Sea Vegetables

Irish Moss
Dulse
Sea Lettuce
A Tangle of Kelps: Sugar Kelp, Winged Kelp, Oar Kelp

Seaweeds are types of algae that grow within and below the intertidal zone of our coastlines throughout eastern Canada. Many of us might politely decline an offer of algae, but edible seaweeds are slowly gaining their due recognition on our dinner tables. Of course, we are only catching up with those who've enjoyed seaweeds for millennia, including many European and Asian cultures.

Edible seaweeds are known for their nutrients and dietary fibre. Some edible seaweeds, including various species of kelp, also contain high levels of glutamates—the flavour-enhancing compound that gives an umami (savoury) taste to dishes. Many edible seaweeds are added to recipes for this reason. The Japanese dashi soup is one example.

What *are* algae? Algae are a group of organisms unto themselves, distinct from plants, animals, and fungi. As seaweeds, algae are plant-like except they have no roots, leaves, or true stems. Marine-based algae fall into three groups: red (such as dulse), green (such as sea lettuce), and brown (such as sugar kelp).

Our coastlines are home to a diversity of seaweeds, including many of the same or similar seaweeds that are eaten in other parts of the world. Although some are hardly edible, not one ocean-growing seaweed is reported to be poisonous as far as my research tells me. One caution is to avoid polluted waters—for obvious reasons. The other caution is that seaweeds, especially some of the brown seaweeds, contain a lot of iodine. We need iodine but excessive amounts can cause troubles and people vary in their sensitivity to it. Enjoy seaweeds, but it may be best to consider them as snacks and flavourings rather than the main dish. Fortunately, dulse, which I can eat a lot of in one sitting, and nori (sushi wrapping) have relatively low amounts of iodine. In addition to their culinary delights, seaweeds (particularly the rockweeds that cover many intertidal areas) are often added to composts or directly to gardens in the fall to build healthy soil.

Many seaweeds are cast upon the beach by storms and can be gathered there if found immediately following the storm. Otherwise, seaweeds must be gathered at low tide. Some seaweeds grow above the low-tide mark and are easily gathered while walking on the seafloor at low tide. Others grow below the low-tide mark and require reaching into the water or accessing them with a kayak or other small boat. In any event, be not afraid of the seaweed. Sally boldly to the coast and engage the world of culinary algae.

Irish Moss (*Chondrus crispus*)

Irish moss may look a little moss-like but it is not moss at all. Irish moss is a type of red algae—yes, a seaweed—that grows close to the low-tide level. It's low-growing, only a few centimetres high, and is highly forked. It ranges in colour from dark to light purple to green to yellowish, and it bleaches white when washed up on the beach and exposed to the sun.

To find it, explore the lowest portions of the coastline at low tide, either on foot or by small boat. It can be picked any time of year. Tide levels change throughout the month and the year, so it can be useful to consult tide charts for the lower tides. Just get on the Internet and search for tide charts then navigate to your section of the coastline (timing of tides change from place to place). There are two low tides every day, so if you miss one there's always another roughly twelve hours later.

There's another, easier way to collect Irish moss. Strong winds and waves often break loose large amounts of Irish moss (and other seaweeds too) and toss it on the beach. Simply walk the beach after a good storm and pick up the windfall. Of course, whenever treading close to the ocean be wary of waves and keep your distance, especially when walking on slippery rocks. Remember too to gather only freshly storm-tossed Irish moss and other seaweeds.

Irish moss has been collected for centuries at least. Today it's used in numerous food and personal care products from ice cream to toothpaste. Irish moss and other similar seaweeds contain carrageenan, which is a spectacular gelling agent. To make vegetarian gelatin simply boil a handful of Irish moss in water for ten minutes and then strain out the moss. The water will gel as it cools. Experiment with different ratios of Irish moss to water for different consistencies of gelatin and store refrigerated. Irish moss can be eaten itself once boiled for a few minutes or can be added to soups and stews to thicken them.

Blancmange is a traditional Irish dessert made by heating whole milk (or as whole as you can get) and Irish moss in a pot for about half an hour (avoid boiling and stir often), then straining the liquid through a sieve (pressing out whatever liquid you can) and adding sugar or honey and various flavourings such as lemon zest, ginger, vanilla, and fruit or berries as you like. Adding a little whiskey or brandy may not be a bad idea. Use roughly half a cup of packed Irish moss per litre of milk, although you may need to experiment to get the desired consistency. You can use either freshly gathered Irish moss or moss that you've dried and stored.

However you decide to use Irish moss and whether it's fresh or dried, be sure to first soak it in fresh water for fifteen minutes and give it a few rinses in running water. This removes its sea flavour that one may not want in one's dessert.

Dulse (*Palmaria palmata*)
a.k.a. Rhodymenia palmata

Dulse is the one seaweed that I grew up eating. It's a popular sea product where I am from in New Brunswick and I find it as addictive as potato chips. Once I start into a bag I find my hand going for more long after I figure I've had enough. Salty and a little chewy with a good dose of umami, dulse makes an excellent snack, especially on a summer afternoon with a glass of beer. Full of trace elements, several vitamins, and protein, it's been a favourite food of those living around the North Atlantic for centuries.

Dulse is a red algae that grows a little above and a little below the low-water mark and is sometimes found cast ashore near the high-tide mark after storms. It has thin and smooth irregularly branched fronds that are attached to the seafloor by a short stem. The fronds are light to dark reddish burgundy, although their colour sometimes fades during summer months, and are about thirty centimetres or less in length and three to ten centimetres in width. Once collected, lay it out in the sun until dry (half a day to several days), then store in paper bags. You can dry on low heat in an oven too.

Dulse is usually eaten dried but not cooked. You can also eat it straight from the sea but might find it a little on the rubbery side. If you see a bit of a powdery white on your dried dulse, fear not; it's just sea salt at no extra price. To mix things up try lightly toasting dulse in the oven or on the stovetop until it turns brittle and crispy. The taste changes too. If you're not a fan of dried dulse, toasted dulse may win you over. It's worth a try. In her book *Spuds! Dulse! Fiddleheads! A Cook's Guide to Maritime Foods,* Judith Comfort recommends sautéing dulse with kale: sauté a diced onion in butter until translucent then add six cups of kale and one cup of shredded dulse and stir and cook until the kale is bright green. You can add dulse to soups, stews, and chowders to add and enhance flavours. If you're a vegetarian, try adding dulse to a pot of baked beans in place of pork; or add it in addition to the pork if you aren't vegetarian.

Sea Lettuce (*Ulva* spp.)

This tissue-thin membranous green algae seems too fragile to survive punishing ocean waves, yet you'll find it in tidal pools and just below the low-tide mark. Light to vibrant green and nearly translucent, sea lettuce fronds are easily identifiable. They grow in wide, irregular sheets, usually less than thirty centimetres long.

Add a little raw sea lettuce to your salad or cook it in a soup or any other savoury dish. Once dried, sea lettuce is brittle and crumbles for easy storage in a glass jar or paper bag.

A Tangle of Kelps

Eastern Canada is home to a number of kelp species, many of which are collected for food. They grow mainly below the low-tide mark and are often cast ashore by storms. Generally not eaten raw, kelps are usually added either fresh or dried to soups or other dishes to bring out savoury flavours, and a little goes a long way. Dry kelp fronds in an oven with low heat or hang them on a clothesline—this method has the added benefit of inviting conversation with your neighbours.

Sugar Kelp (*Saccharina latissima*) is a brown algae with long (up to four metres) undivided and frilly fronds with no mid-rib. Add it to soups for both a savoury and slightly sweet taste, or fry it for a crispy and tasty snack food. When it dries you may see a white powder form. Worry not. Put a little on your tongue for a salty-sweet treat. It's a combination of salt and a type of sugar produced by the kelp.

Winged Kelp (*Alaria esculenta*), also known as badderlocks, edible kelp, and wakame, is another brown algae that grows at or just below the low-tide mark on rocky, exposed shorelines. Its yellowish to greenish undivided narrow fronds can grow two to five metres in length and have conspicuous mid-ribs and wavy edges. To eat, boil it for ten minutes or so then add to salads or serve as a side dish. You can also toast it in the oven or in a pan for a few minutes until it's crispy. Its Latin name attests to its culinary history: *esculenta* means "edible" and *alaria* means "wing."

Oar Kelp (*Laminaria digitata*), also known as fingered kelp or horsetail kelp, is a brown algae with long (up to three metres) branched dark-brown fronds attached to the sea-bottom with distinctive stems (stipe is the technical term). It grows on exposed rocky coastlines at and below the low-tide mark. Add it fresh or dried to soups or fry or bake it to make kelp chips.

Oar kelp

Pollock and cranberries

I n addition to plants and seaweeds, our shorelines offer a feast of easily gathered or caught seafood. Snails, bivalves, and close-to-shore fish can be had with a bit of knowledge and a minimal amount of gear.

A word of caution

Bivalves (clams, mussels, oysters, and scallops) are filter feeders and can become contaminated with pollutants and naturally occurring toxic organisms that cause paralytic shellfish poisoning. Some toxins can occur year-round, and some are more common during summer months. These toxins can cause gastrointestinal discomfort and even (though rarely) death. Before collecting bivalves you should check with the Department of Fisheries and Oceans (DFO) to determine whether shellfish are safe to collect in your area. DFO closes and opens sections of coastline from time to time (sometimes for one or several shellfish, sometimes for all shellfish) so it's necessary to double check with them before you forage. Collecting shellfish in closed areas is illegal.

The recreational harvest of many shellfish is subject to additional regulations beyond closed and open beaches. There is no recreational fishery for lobster, for example, and collecting scallops requires a recreational scallop licence and you must report your catch. Collecting oysters also requires a licence and as no new licences are currently being issued, foraging oysters is essentially not possible at present. For these reasons lobster, oysters, and scallops are not included in this book.

Periwinkle (*Littorina littorea*)
a.k.a. Winkle

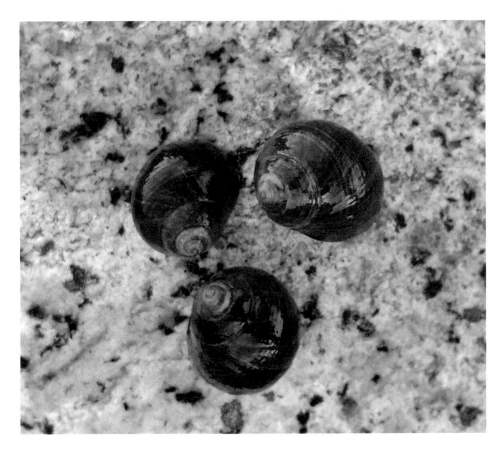

I love to gather a few dozen periwinkles while walking on a beach with friends who've never eaten them, and then offer them as hors d'oeuvres that evening. Often reticent at first, most people take a liking to periwinkles once they try these gastronomical gastropods.

Now ubiquitous along our coast, periwinkles are not native to eastern Canada but rather showed up on our shores in the mid-1800s, likely as hitchhikers on ships. They mostly feed on algae and so do not have the same toxin concerns as the filter-feeding bivalves do. They are found throughout the intertidal zone with the largest ones sometimes occurring near the lower end of this zone. Periwinkles have a thick, hard shell and a circular dark disk—the operculum—that serves as a door of sorts when the periwinkle retreats inside its shell.

Humans have eaten periwinkles for millennia, which we know from periwinkle shells found preserved in ancient people's kitchen middens. Beyond their fine taste, periwinkles are rich in protein and omega-3 fatty acids. Although more popular on the east side of the North Atlantic, "winkles" are commercially collected by "winklers" along Canada's east coast as well, and most of them exported. No licence is required to collect periwinkles and there are no restrictions except that they must be collected by hand rather than by mechanical means. So, as they say, fill yer boots. It's worth passing over the small ones to search out the largest. Commercial winklers pass their catch over a mesh screen in order to retain only the larger ones.

I like to boil periwinkles in seawater whenever possible, and if not I'll salt the water before boiling. Five to ten minutes is enough. Once cooked the operculum falls off easily and the meat can be picked out of the shell with a pin, hawthorn's thorn, toothpick, or similar sharp object. Many like to dip their periwinkles (once picked from the shell) in melted butter, sometimes laced with garlic, but I find them tasty and rich enough on their own. Usually I enjoy a dozen or two for an hors d'oeuvre and leave it at that, but occasionally I'm patient enough (or a companion is patient enough) to pick out a pile of cooked periwinkle meats to add to a pasta. It's worth the effort.

Perhaps my interest in periwinkles began with Dennis Lee's poem "Periwinkle Pizza," in which he proclaims that he will eat his supper with relish if given periwinkle pizza in St. Andrews By-the-Sea, which happens to be my hometown. My mother actually went through the trouble of making me a periwinkle pizza when I was a kid after we read that poem.

Northern Shortfin Squid (*Illex illecebrosus*)

Photo by Dave Adler

Returning from the town pub one night, my mother and a friend happened to look over the seawall to the beach below where they spied hundreds of washed-ashore squid. Fuelled by the evening's libations, they grabbed some garbage bags and filled them with the seafood windfall. They took most of the squid to another friend who runs a local restaurant and, so the story goes, calamari was on the menu for at least a week.

Squid are mysterious and short-lived creatures. Most live less than a year and they share their evolutionary history with snails and other mollusks. The thin and translucent cartilage cuttlebone within their body is the only remnant of their ancestral shell. Although scientists know that they migrate from deep offshore waters to shallower near-shore waters in late spring, and do the reverse in the fall, no one knows exactly where they go to have their young. Squid eggs have never been found in the wild, and scientists also do not know how deep they swim, although they have been found at depths of a kilometre. Squid are believed to die within a few days of spawning.

Squid are usually reddish brown on their upper side and white or pale pink on their underside, but they can change their colour in a flash to match their surroundings. When you pull one out of the water with a fishing rod you can watch it pulse though various colours. Known as cephalopods, squid have ten "arms" equipped with suckers, two of which are distinctly longer than the others and are often called tentacles. Using a jet propulsion system, squid dart forward and backward with surprising speed as they swim in large schools hunting for prey. Our North Atlantic species of squid grows to only about thirty centimetres in length.

Squid tend to come close to shore and close to the surface at night to feed. At a wedding party in Halifax one night I looked over the railing and saw hundreds of ghostly white shapes cruising in formation though the water below, illuminated by outdoor lights. A few nights later, around midnight, friends and I stole back to that dock with fishing rods and squid lures and left with a bagful.

Squid can be caught while deep-sea fishing using a special squid jig, but I usually catch them when they come in close to shore at night. Arriving at a dock or wharf in the middle of the night is delightfully eerie. But you likely won't be alone. If the squid are running, you'll find a handful of dedicated squid fishers quietly casting their lures. In my experience, squid are finicky so it's best to have a few colours of squid lures to try. If you see a fellow squid fisher getting lucky, you might try sneaking a look at her lure. Timing is important too. You may see dozens of squid swimming about and not one will go for your lure until the clock strikes just the right hour of night. Make sure to have a bucket or bag at the ready. Squid sometimes squirt ink when they're caught, which can make for a messy dock in a hurry.

To clean squid, start by pulling the head from the body, which will pull the innards from the body as well. Cut the head away from the arms (keeping the arms themselves connected) and discard it and the innards. Make sure to remove and discard the hard cartilage beak from the base of the arms too. I've yet to try using the ink from the squid's ink sac but you can find recipes that call for it. Next, remove the thin, translucent piece of cartilage known as the cuttlebone from the body by pulling it free. If you are not looking to make squid rings, then you can cut the body lengthwise with scissors to make removing the cuttlebone easier. Some people remove the skin next but I like to leave it on to maintain the colour.

As a child my first taste of squid was prepared by a family friend who fried the body rings, tail, and arms in a light batter heavy with curry spices. I can't think of squid without remembering the smell of curried calamari filling the kitchen. With or without curry spices and with or without a light batter, squid are excellent fried over high heat for no more than a few minutes. You can also add squid to soups or chowders provided you simmer them long enough to ensure the squid becomes tender.

In 1928, fifteen-year-old Arthur Scammell of Change Islands, Newfoundland, wrote "Squid Jiggin' Ground," a song recounting local fishermen's excitement at the first run of squid. I had the pleasure of hiking the Squid Jiggers Trail once while visiting friends on Change Islands. Here's sample of Scammell's song:

There's men from the Harbour, there's men from the Tickle
In all kinds of motorboats, green, grey and brown.
Right yonder there's Bobby and with him is Noddy,
He's chawing hard tack on the squid jiggin' ground.

Holy smoke! What a scuffle, all hands are excited.
'Tis a wonder to me that there's nobody drowned.
There's confusion, a bustle, a wonderful hustle.
They're all jigging squids on the squid jiggin' ground.

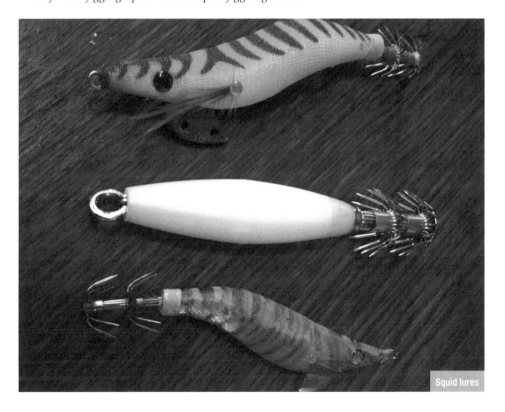

Squid lures

Soft-Shell Clam (*Mya arenaria*)
a.k.a. Steamers, Longnecks

Soft-shell clams were a staple for Indigenous peoples of coastal eastern North America for countless generations. I often pause while walking beaches near my hometown in New Brunswick to pick up a bit of shell from one of the extensive clam-shell middens and try to picture the Passamaquoddy person who dug, cooked, and ate that clam, at that very spot. What did she think about? Did her children play on these very rocks?

Soft-shell clams are a popular food all down the eastern seaboard and commercial clammers dig hundreds of tonnes of clams for sale every year. No licence is needed for recreational digging, although you're limited by regulation to between one hundred and three hundred clams per day depending on where you are digging (check with the Department of Fisheries and Oceans [DFO] for details). You can only keep clams larger than forty-four millimetres (about an inch and three-quarters, measured lengthwise) unless you're on Nova Scotia's eastern shore where the minimum size is fifty millimetres. Only handheld tools are allowed. Don't forget to check with DFO to determine whether a particular area is free of toxins and open for digging.

Soft-shell clams live buried in the seabed within the intertidal zone at depths varying from several to about twenty centimetres. I've dug clams using my bare hands, small trowels, shovels, garden forks, and specially designed clamming hoes. As their name suggests, the shells are easily broken and it is heartbreaking to see a beautiful large clam broken by the shovel, rendering it pretty much worthless for food because of the sand that inevitably fills in. It takes some practice to dig clams efficiently and without breaking too many. Sometimes smaller tools and hands are the best option if you don't have a clamming hoe.

How to find them if they're underground? Each clam has a telltale hole on the surface through which it breathes and eats. If you don't see any right away, get down close to the seabed and look hard. They can be difficult to spot at first but you'll soon develop a knack for spotting clam holes and will be impressing your friends in no time.

For me there's no better way to cook clams than to bake them on a beach with a crowd of friends. Friends of mine have held an annual clambake for some forty years now, and I've attended about thirty of them. (See the directions for a clambake on the next page.) Aside from the traditional clambake, I like to boil my clams in seawater (or salted water if necessary) for ten minutes or so until the clams open up and then another couple of minutes for good measure. Save the cooking water and pour some into a bowl. To eat, pull the two shells apart and pluck out the meat. Grip the clam at the base of its neck and pull the rough covering off the neck. Then, give the clam a good swish in the hot cooking water to flush out any remaining grit. If you've got a batch of clams that are particularly gritty, run your thumb along the inner edge of the clam's body to rid it of hidden grit. Dipping in melted butter is good, although I prefer just a swish in the hot, salty cooking water. Note: Gritty clams are a sure way to turn people off clams. A good wash post-digging and leaving the live clams in a bucket of water overnight helps reduce the grit before they're cooked. Some people suggest adding cornmeal to the water for the clams to take up and displace their grit.

How to Bake Clams on a Beach

Here's how to do a clambake. Start digging a pit on the beach around eight-o'clock in the morning for a midday feast. Be sure you know when and how high the tide will come in and choose your spot accordingly. You'll need about four or five hours of tide-free beach. The pit should be about a metre wide, a half metre deep, and about a metre to a metre and a half long. Get a roaring bonfire going in the pit and once the fire is in full swing start adding fist- to softball-sized rocks to the fire. Keep adding wood to keep the fire going, too. While the fire is burning, send kids and adventurous adults on a mission to collect fresh rockweed. People might be a little shy at first but if you invited the right sort of people, more than likely they will soon be hugging and lugging armloads of the stuff. Have them make a good-sized pile beside the fire.

Let the fire burn down after an hour or two and remove any remaining unburned wood. If you've added enough rocks and burned the fire long enough you'll have an even bed of super-hot rocks about fifteen to thirty centimetres deep in the bottom of the pit. Use a rake if necessary to ensure a flat bed of rocks. Now, toss handfuls of fresh, wet seaweed on the hot rocks to cover them five to eight centimetres deep. Hissing, billowing clouds of steam are what you want. Look for any seaweed that turns a bright green and cover these spots with a few handfuls more of rockweed.

Next, spread a layer of cheesecloth over the steaming rockweed and pile on an even layer of clams, quartered raw potatoes, peeled onions, and whatever other foods you'd like to bake. Follow this with another layer of cheesecloth, then a few more centimetres of rockweed, and finally a canvas tarp or old sheet. Use the last of the rockweed to seal the edges of the tarp or sheet. Now sit back, open a beer, or play a game of softball or Frisbee, and wait about an hour. Pull back the tarp, rockweed, and top layer of cheesecloth and, if all went well, you'll reveal a perfectly cooked feast of onions, potatoes, and clams. A clambake can take a little practice. My friends joke that after a few decades we're finally getting it more or less right.

Razor Clam (*Ensis directus*)
a.k.a. Atlantic Jackknife Clam

The razor clam I know looks like an old-fashioned straight razor and is sometimes known as the jackknife clam. There is another species of clam called razor clam (*Siliqua costata*), and while it is perfectly edible it is not as common in my experience and so not included in this book.

Razor clams live in colonies in sand and mud flats in intertidal and subtidal areas. They burrow themselves into the sand or mud, coming to the surface usually only to feed when the tide is in. Although I've never seen it, razor clams are apparently adept swimmers. They accomplish this feat by sucking water in one end of their shells and jetting it out the other.

To find them, look for their empty shells strewn along beaches as your first clue. Then, search out their breathing and feeding holes in the mud or sand, which are often shaped like an old-fashioned keyhole. The hunt gets trickier from here. If you find soft-shelled clams too easy a prey then perhaps you're ready for the razor clam. Grab your garden fork or clam hoe and quickly yet gently remove the top ten or fifteen centimetres of mud. If you're lucky you'll see the top portion of the clam sticking up from where you dug. Be nimble, be quick, and snatch ahold of the clam and slowly pull it up out of the sand. Razor clams burrow deep into the mud with an alarming speed, so if you don't get them quickly they'll soon disappear out of reach.

Once you've pulled them from the sand, put them in a basket or bucket. Those left on the beach will do their best to escape back down into the mud. You may gasp a little when you see the razor clam extend its foot, which approaches the length of its shell, in search of mud in which to burrow.

Little luck with the razor clam hunt? Here's a trick: Bring a box of table salt and a container of water with you to the beach. When you find the razor clam holes, alternate pouring in salt and a little water until, well, I'll let you see for yourself. Search "salt, razor clams, catch" on the Internet for a preview.

There is no size limit for razor clams, but it makes sense to bring home only the largest. Regulations permit recreational diggers to collect between one hundred and three hundred clams per day (total of all species collected), depending on the region. Check with the Department of Fisheries and Oceans for details.

Razor clams can be cooked like any other clam, although a popular method is to cook them in butter, in their shells, on the stovetop.

Quahog (*Mercenaria mercenaria*)
a.k.a. Cherrystone, Chowder Clam, Hard-Shell Clam, Littleneck

Quahogs have long been a food source along the eastern North American seaboard. They were a staple for Indigenous people who not only ate them but also made wampum from their shells, which was used as jewellery and currency. The Pilgrims supposedly were saved from starvation when shown how to collect these clams by the local Indigenous people.

Quahogs can grow up to about ten centimetres wide, and their common names often correspond to their size. The smallest are littlenecks, then come the cherrystones, and the largest are sometimes known as chowders. In eastern Canada, quahogs must be at least 3.8 centimetres (an inch and a half) to be legally collected. As with other clams, you may collect between one hundred and three hundred clams total (of all species collected) per day depending on the region, and may use only handheld tools to dig them.

Unlike soft-shell clams, quahogs generally live below the intertidal zone, which means you need to get wet to find them. A common way to collect quahogs is to wade in the water at low tide and slowly shuffle your bare feet through the sand until you feel one. Then reach or dive down and pick it up. With a little practice your toes will soon distinguish quahogs from stones. Pull a mesh sack or a bucket along with you to hold your catch. When you find one quahog you'll usually find a bed of them. Where to start looking? A beach with emptied quahogs is a good place to start. Of course, our cold waters mean a wetsuit is often required for this adventure.

Quahogs can be steamed or boiled and dipped in melted butter or added to chowders. Larger quahogs can be a bit tough so are often cooked in chowder or sometimes cooked until they open and are then chopped and mixed with onions and lemon juice before returning to their shells and baked, covered, for fifteen or twenty minutes.

Blue Mussel (*Mytilus edulis*)
a.k.a. Common Mussel

Blue mussels live in the intertidal and subtidal area, often growing in massive clumps or beds. They usually attach themselves to rocks or each other with surprisingly strong byssal threads that they produce. As their name implies, this species of mussel is often blue but can range from purple to nearly black.

Blue mussels tend to concentrate toxins (whether natural or otherwise) more than other bivalves. For this reason, areas that are open for clam digging may be closed to mussel collecting. Most of the Bay of Fundy area for example is closed to mussel collecting at time of writing.

Provided you can find an area open to mussel collecting, they can be collected in large numbers at low tide from various types of shorelines. Regulations limit your haul to no more than three hundred mussels per day, but surely that's plenty. Unlike clams, mussels are subject to open and closed seasons. Check with the Department of Fisheries and Oceans for the dates in your area.

Mussels are usually steamed, sometimes with various ingredients added to the pot to make a savoury or spicy broth. Wine and cream are common additions. Importantly, check your mussels for pearls! Not for their value but rather to save you from an unplanned visit to your dentist. Pearls I've found range in size from one to several millimetres in size, and each mussel can have multiple pearls embedded within it.

A less common method to cook mussels is known as *éclade de moules*. Arrange your mussels outdoors on a rocky surface or on boards that you don't mind burning and build a fire of dry conifer twigs (no more than a few millimetres in diameter) or dry pine needles over top of them. Take a little time to place the mussels with their hinge side up so that they will open facing down as they cook and more or less avoid filling up with ash. They are done soon after they open, usually within about five minutes or so of total cooking time. Test a mussel from the outer edge of the pile to make sure it's completely cooked. If not, add more pine needles or conifer twigs and repeat the process until they're fully cooked.

I did a version of this once while kayaking on the Bay of Exploits in Newfoundland. The water was surprisingly warm and when my companion and I stopped for lunch, I dove down sans wetsuit (sans anything actually) to collect a few handfuls of mussels. We gathered dried spruce twigs for the fire and enjoyed the touch of smoky, woodsy taste they added to the mussels. Basking in the sun, salt crystallizing on my skin, it was a meal to remember.

Sea Urchin (*Strongylocentrotus droebachiensis*)

Sea urchins are prickly critters that slowly roam the ocean floor, using their spines to both move themselves along and to bring bits of seaweed and other edible detritus to their five-part, beak-like mouths. They can grow to about five or seven centimetres across and their spines are one to two centimetres long.

You might happen upon the delicate, spineless skeletons of sea urchins washed up on a beach or left on rocks by seagulls that sometimes eat them. You can find them alive at low tide in tidal pools or at the base of wharves, or perhaps clustered on the bottom near the low-tide mark when kayaking close to shore. Snorkellers and scuba divers often see large patches of these sea creatures. Urchins are usually harvested in the fall and winter when their edible parts are at their biggest and best.

Sea urchins have been commercially fished in recent decades. They are usually gathered by specially licensed scuba divers and are mostly sold to overseas markets. While hundreds of tonnes of sea urchins are shipped yearly from eastern Canada to foreign buyers, few eastern Canadians are aware of this delicacy and fewer still have tried one.

So be brave, pluck yourself an urchin (being mindful of its sharp spines), crack it open on a rock, and scoop out the yellow or orange "stuff," and savour a unique seafood treat: *uni* or *nama uni*, as it's known in Japanese. Smashing with a rock a little too primal for you? While wearing a leather glove, hold the urchin in your hand while you cut off the bottom of the urchin with a pair of scissors, allow the liquid to drain, and then scoop out the yellow/orange uni with a spoon.

The flavour is somehow both mild and rich, almost sweet and a little salty, kind of like watermelon, and the texture is soft and creamy. Uni can be eaten raw on the spot by itself or heaped on a cracker, baked in the oven in its shell at 450° F for about five minutes, or used to make urchin ceviche (mix with lemon or lime juice, olive oil, and diced onions, and let sit for fifteen to thirty minutes).

A Trio of Ocean Fish: Mackerel (*Scomber scombrus*), Pollock (*Pollachius* sp.) a.k.a. Pollack, and Flounder (various species)

You might assume you need a boat to go ocean fishing, but not so. In many parts of eastern Canada good fishing can be had from wharves and docks and sometimes right from shore. A spin-casting rod outfitted with a sinker, hook, and a clam for bait is all that is required to catch a flounder. For mackerel no bait is needed so long as you have a mackerel lure, which will also catch pollock just fine. And unlike freshwater fishing, no licence is required to catch these fish. Of course, rules change with time so it may be worth checking local regulations just to be sure.

I didn't have many rules as a kid but one I do remember, and it seemed harsh at the time, is that I wasn't allowed on the town wharf by myself until I was ten years old. From the shore at high tide I caught a few harbour pollock, as we called the very young pollock that found their way close to shore, and bore the advice of passersby that I might have better luck fishing from the wharf. Following my tenth birthday I made up for lost time and spent a good part of my summers on the wharf, fishing for flounder and harbour pollock.

Photo by Amy Weston

The necessary gear to catch a flounder is basic: a spin-casting fishing rod, a hook, a sinker (weight), and some sort of bait. I used soft-shell clams that I dug at low tide next to the wharf where I fished as a kid. Either the sinker or the hook can be attached to the end of the line. I always put hook first, but many go with sinker first. Either way, the sinker should be about twenty to thirty centimetres from the hook. Because flounder live on the bottom and tend to not move around much, it makes sense to cast your line out as far as you can, let it sink to the bottom, and then gradually reel it in, slowly pulling the hook and sinker across the bottom. This can be a good way to get a hook stuck, but in the right areas this seems not to happen often.

Here's a more primal way to secure a flounder: try spearing one. Flounder spearing was once a common practice, done at low tide from a small boat. Flounders change their colouring to match the surrounding sea floor so spotting them can be challenging. A friend and I once decided to see if we could catch a flounder while snorkelling. We whittled makeshift spears from a couple of alder stems and swam out with wetsuits, masks, and snorkels. We each had a chance at one. I missed but my friend proved nimble with his alder-stick spear, and we swam back to shore with one good-sized flounder. We supplemented our supper that evening with flounder fillets cooked in butter over a campfire.

Mackerel and pollock can be caught from small boats, wharves, and even from shore in some places. Travelling in large schools, these fish feed close to shore during summer months before heading for deeper waters in winter. "Are the mackerel running yet?" is a common question along the coast. I find that both mackerel and pollock can be fished from July to nearly the end of September.

I have a few spots along the shore within an hour's drive of Halifax where I catch a few good meals of mackerel (and sometimes pollock) every summer. Not long ago a companion and I camped overnight at one such spot, enjoying a star-filled night sky. In the morning, a few casts landed us a breakfast of mackerel that we cooked over a

wood fire on a metal grill while we sipped coffee and watched the morning sunlight catch on the ocean's ripples.

Fresh out of the water with a touch of salt and lemon juice if you want (although none needed really), mackerel is one of the finest fish I've tasted. Mackerel is also a very nutritious food, high in omega-3 fatty acids among other nutrients, and fortunately contains much less mercury than many of the ocean fish we eat.

With a bit of practice you can learn to peel the backbone and most of the fine bones out of a cooked mackerel, leaving behind the skin and the rich, almost sweet, flesh. Mackerel have a lot of fat. This makes them tasty when fresh and less than pleasant if left too long before cooking. If someone disparages mackerel, I'll bet they haven't had fresh mackerel. Introduce such a person to a mackerel cooked over a wood fire on a beach soon after catching and they'll never speak ill of mackerel again.

Pollock have much less fat than mackerel. They are fine eating, but I sometimes return them to the ocean in hopes of landing a mackerel for dinner instead. Pollock can grow much larger than mackerel but only the small ones come close to shore. The pollock and mackerel I catch are usually close to the same size and are less than thirty centimetres in length.

A good way to catch mackerel (and pollock) is to use a mackerel rig, which you can find at fishing supply stores. A metre in length and containing up to six hooks, casting these unwieldy rigs can take some practice. But they are effective. Perhaps too effective, as I sometimes catch three or four fish at once—all I want to eat—quickly bringing the fishing to an end. A regular spinner lure can work just fine too.

An Interview with George Smith, Dancing River Sprite

A few evenings each month, adventurous diners have a chance to attend a special gathering at an old pink farmhouse in Middle River, Cape Breton. George and his wife, Cora-Lee Eisses-Smith, offer their guests a multi-course meal creatively built on a different book each month, and recently celebrated their one-hundredth book-dinner. The literary choices are nothing if not diverse. Past dinners have featured Daphne Du Maurier's *Rebecca*, Rudyard Kipling's short story "The Gate of a Hundred Sorrows," Jack Finney's *Time and Again*, and Hans Christian Andersen's *The Princess and the Pea*. George often features food foraged from nearby forests and fields.

The book might not have anything to do with food. Rather, we interpret what sort of food might fit the theme of the book. We have menus for each month's meal, but part of the fun is that we write them cryptically, so our guests don't always know what they'll be eating, but they have fun trying to decipher the clues, which are all based on the book that we feature for that month.

During pauses between courses, Cora-Lee reads passages from the book and I talk about the food we're serving. How I grew, acquired or raised it, or where I foraged for it.

A favourite use of wild foods is flavouring the marinade I use when curing hams and bacon with spruce tips and juniper berries. You need to work carefully with the flavours of wild foods. It's not predictable like adding salt; it can be a little different every time.

I like to gather blossoms from wild apple trees, and chanterelles and fiddleheads of course. Ground ivy (a.k.a. creeping Charlie) is so abundant and hardy, sometimes I even get a little of it from under the snow. I deep-fry dandelion flowers in a tempura batter, and pickle some of our fiddleheads, and I once made a crème-brûlée with chanterelles too. That was very interesting. Sometimes I juice spruce tips to make a spruce tip and rhubarb salsa.

I do get a lot of customers who are wild food first-timers. I add wildflowers to some dishes, and have to remind guests that they are edible or else they might leave behind a daisy or purple vetch or evening primrose uneaten. It's a bit of an adventure for them.

Wherever we go we forage. I just enjoy getting out for a walk, and seeing what's available any given day.

Dancing River Sprite
Cora-Lee Eisses
ceisses@ns.sympatico.ca

Photo by Shawn Dunlop, Lakeside Photography

Huckleberries

Crowberries and juniper berries

Bibliography

Angier, Bradford. *How to Eat in the Woods: A Complete Guide to Foraging, Trapping, Fishing, and Finding Sustenance in the Wild.* Black Dog and Leventhal Publishers: New York, NY. 2016.

Blouin, Glen. *Weeds of the Woods: Small Trees and Shrubs of the Eastern Forest, Second Edition.* Nimbus Publishing: Halifax, NS. 2012.

Comfort, Judith. *Spuds! Dulse! Fiddleheads! A Cook's Guide to Maritime Foods.* Nimbus Publishing Limited: Halifax, NS. 1986.

Derevitzky, Catherine. *Lobster Pots and Searocket Sandwiches.* Down East Books: Camden ME. 1979.

Drake, Kitty and Ned Pratt. *Rabbit Ravioli: Photographs, Recipes & Literary Vignettes of Newfoundland.* Breakwater: St. John's, NL. 1994.

Gardon, Anne. *The Wild Food Gourmet.* Firefly Books Ltd.: Willowdale, ON. 1998.

Garrett, Blanche Pownall. *A Taste of the Wild.* James Lorimer & Co: Toronto, ON. 1975.

Gibbons, Euell. *Stalking the Wild Asparagus.* A. C. Hood: Putney, VT. 1962.

Gibbons, Euell. *Stalking the Blue-Eyed Scallop.* A. C. Hood: Putney, VT. 1964.

MacLeod, Heather and Barbara MacDonald. *Edible Wild Plants of Nova Scotia.* Nimbus Publishing: Halifax, NS. 1988.

Index

Photo by Dan Hutt

About the author

Jamie Simpson is a forester, lawyer, and writer
with a passion for exploring our natural world
(and sometimes eating it). He is the author of
*Restoring the Acadian Forest: A Guide to Forest
Stewardship for Woodlot Owners in Eastern
Canada*, and *Journeys through Eastern Old-
growth Forests*. Jamie has received several
awards for his conservation work, including the
Elizabeth May Award for Environmental Service,
the *Environmental Law Prize* from Dalhousie
University, and the *Honour in the Woods Award*
from the Nova Scotia Environmental Network.